INFORMATION TECHNOLOGY

OPERATIONS EXCELLENCE

DATA DRIVEN TOOLS & TECHNIQUES FOR TRANSFORMATIVE RESULTS

e k a
PUBLISHING

SHRUTI TYAGI
SWAPNIL SAURAV

Published in USA by Eka Publishers 2025

Copyright © Eka Publishers

Printed and bound by Eka Publishers

Author: Shruti Tyagi & Swapnil Saurav

Editor: Kumari Smriti

Cover Design: Aniruddh Vaidya

1st Print January 2025

EKA PUBLISHERS
#118 Ushodaya Enclave, PO Miyapur
Hyderabad 500049. INDIA
ekapresshyderabad@gmail.com
+91 8008101590
www.ekapress.org

PREFACE

In the age of rapid technological advancement, IT operations stand as the foundation upon which modern businesses are built. Whether ensuring seamless service delivery, maintaining system uptime, or tackling the complexities of incident management, IT operations have become central to every organization's success. Yet, as systems grow more intricate and data volumes surge, the traditional approaches to managing IT infrastructures are reaching their limits.

This book, "IT Operations Excellence: Data-Driven Tools and Techniques for Transformative Results", is born out of a simple yet profound realization: the future of IT operations lies in leveraging the transformative power of data and machine learning. The integration of these tools doesn't just offer a marginal improvement—it represents a paradigm shift in how organizations approach efficiency, resilience, and problem management.

In crafting this book, we aimed to address a critical gap in the knowledge landscape. While much has been written about the technical intricacies of machine learning and the operational nuances of IT management, few resources bring these domains together in a practical, actionable way. This book seeks to bridge that gap by guiding readers through the application of machine learning algorithms to real-world IT challenges.

Each chapter of this book delves into a specific problem commonly encountered in IT operations—from predicting system downtimes to Security Threat Detection and Proactive Problem Management. Using actual data scenarios, the book demonstrates how machine learning can transform these challenges into opportunities for proactive and efficient management. Readers will not only learn the theory behind algorithms but will also gain hands-on experience in applying them to practical problems, ensuring that knowledge is both meaningful and actionable.

This book is intended for IT professionals, data enthusiasts, and business leaders alike—anyone who seeks to harness the potential of AI and machine learning in IT operations. It is written to be accessible to those with a foundational understanding of IT systems and data analysis, yet it also offers deeper insights that will challenge and inspire seasoned practitioners.

As you progress through the chapters, you'll encounter real-world data, intuitive explanations of machine learning techniques, and step-by-step guides to solving IT-specific problems. By the end, you'll not only have a firm grasp of the technical aspects but also a clear vision of how to implement data-driven strategies in your organization.

The journey to creating this book has been as rewarding as the destination. It has been shaped by insights gained from countless conversations with IT leaders, data scientists, and operations teams who face these challenges daily. Their stories, struggles, and triumphs have informed the examples, case studies, and solutions presented within these pages.

This book is more than a guide; it is a call to action. It challenges organizations to move beyond traditional IT management and embrace a future where systems are smarter, decisions are data-driven, and operations are more resilient. With machine learning, we have the tools to not only meet today's challenges but also anticipate and prepare for the demands of tomorrow.

Thank you for embarking on this journey with us. We sincerely hope this book inspires you to innovate, experiment, and unlock the transformative potential of AI-powered IT operations.

SHRUTI TYAGI
SWAPNIL SAURAV

GITHUB LOCATION FOR THE DATA:
All the dataset mentioned in this book can be downloaded from:
https://github.com/swapnilsaurav/ITOpExcellence

ABOUT THE AUTHOR

Shruti is a seasoned technology leader with over 15 years of global experience in IT operations, specializing in data science, Machine Learning, generative AI, and SaaS.Her expertise lies in leveraging data-driven strategies and advanced technologies to drive efficiency, resilience, and operational excellence in IT systems.

Shruti's deep understanding of IT operations and data science allows her to bridge the gap between technical intricacies and business needs, enabling organizations to unlock the full potential of AI and Machine Learning in IT management. Through her work, she has guided teams and organizations in utilizing Machine Learning algorithms to tackle real-world challenges, from system downtime prediction to proactive problem management.

As the author of this book Shruti shares her knowledge and experience in applying Machine Learning to improve IT operations, offering practical insights that empower IT professionals, data enthusiasts, and business leaders to create smarter, more resilient systems.

Beyond her professional accomplishments, Shruti balances her dynamic career with her role as a devoted mother of two young children.

ABOUT THE AUTHOR

Swapnil Saurav is an established management professional, tech enthusiast, and lifelong learner. Saurav showcases over 20 years of expertise in the development of enterprise applications, which is bolstered by his competitive business acumen and deep understanding of customer challenges. This has equipped him to drive exceptional business growth in fiercely competitive market standings. His proficiencies extend across various business sectors such as CPG, Retail, Supply Chain Management and Healthcare Industries. He possesses an in-depth understanding of process consulting, market analysis, product development, and project management. His ability to navigate complex business landscapes is further enhanced by his innovative thinking and problem-solving prowess, attributes that have been instrumental in developing groundbreaking enterprise solutions.

Additionally, to his professional success, Saurav holds patents and is an author of multiple books on Technology and Management. Saurav's patents are in the areas of Artificial Intelligence. He has written books on Python Programming, SQL Programming, Machine Learning, Artificial Intelligence, Data Visualization, Retail Management, and Supply Chain Management. He has been invited by various technical and management colleges in India to speak on the latest technologies and management trends. Saurav holds an MBA from SP Jain Institute of Management & Research (Mumbai, India), an MTech from BITS Pilani (Pilani, India), with Bachelor's degree in Computer Science & Engineering (VTU, Belgaum, India). He is currently pursuing PhD from GITAM University (Hyderabad, India) in the areas of Augmented Reality.

—•○◇○•—

ABOUT THE EDITOR

Smriti is a storyteller, editor, aptitude and soft skills trainer, marketing professional and an entrepreneur. Smriti has BTech degree from JNTUCEH and PGDM from IIM Lucknow. She has almost two decades of work experience spanning across Technology and Education sectors. Her journey through these roles has allowed her to meet and work with people with diverse backgrounds, education, geographies and experiences. This has helped her understand and capture stories, styles, psychology, practices, enthusiasm and creativity from a vast array of people.

An entrepreneur by profession, Smriti has found a passion in telling and re-telling of stories of people: those who can spin their stories into words easily to those who may need support to reach a wider audience and everyone in between. She recognizes the shortcomings, and equally appreciates the strength of writers, students and readers. Capturing their essence and emotions in words.

——————•○◇○•——————

TABLE OF CONTENT

Chapter 1
Setting The Stage For Data-Driven It Operations   03

Chapter 2
Predicting System Downtime Using Historical Logs   31

Chapter 3
Anomaly Detection For Real-Time Monitoring   61

Chapter 4
Root Cause Analysis Using Log Classification   101

Chapter 5
Incident Categorization Using NLP   129

Chapter 6
Security Threat Detection Using Behavioral Analytics   155

Chapter 7
Proactive Problem Management With Predictive Insights   185

Chapter 8
Comprehensive IT Operations   205

Setting The Stage For
Data-Driven It Operations

CHAPTER 1

SETTING THE STAGE FOR DATA-DRIVEN IT OPERATIONS

1.1 The Evolution of IT Operations

IT operations have undergone a remarkable transformation over the decades, driven by advancements in technology, changing business needs, and the exponential growth of data. To understand the significance of data-driven IT operations today, it is essential to trace the historical journey of IT operations, from its manual origins to its current data-centric state.

The Early Days: Manual and Reactive Operations

In the early stages of IT operations, systems were simpler, and the volume of data being processed was relatively small. Operations were largely manual and reactive, focusing on troubleshooting issues as they arose, rather than preventing them.

- **Key Characteristics**:
    - Minimal automation: System administrators relied on manual logs and physical inspections.
    - Reactive approach: Problems were addressed only after they occurred, often leading to downtime.
    - Limited scalability: Growing IT demands strained manual processes, causing inefficiencies.
    - Lack of insights: Operational decisions were made based on experience rather than data.

For example, if a server crashed, IT teams would manually inspect logs and attempt to identify the root cause. This process was time-consuming and prone to human error, often resulting in prolonged system outages.

The Rise of Automation: Streamlining Operations

With the advent of automation tools in the 1990s and early 2000s, IT operations began to shift from manual interventions to automated workflows. This period marked a significant leap forward in operational efficiency.

- **Key Developments**:
    - ○ **Monitoring tools**: Tools like Nagios and Zabbix provided real-time insights into system performance.
    - ○ **Automated scripts**: Tasks like backups, updates, and patches were automated, reducing the need for constant manual intervention.
    - ○ **Improved reliability**: Automation helped minimize human errors and accelerated routine tasks.

This era saw the birth of monitoring dashboards and alert systems, allowing IT teams to identify potential issues before they escalated. However, the approach was still predominantly reactive, as alerts were triggered only after performance thresholds were breached.

The Advent of Proactive Operations

The increasing complexity of IT systems and the rise of distributed architectures highlighted the need for a more proactive approach to operations. By the mid-2000s, businesses began to adopt proactive monitoring and predictive analytics.

- **Key Characteristics**:
    - ○ **Predictive maintenance**: Using historical data to forecast potential failures.
    - ○ **Centralized monitoring**: Unified dashboards provided a single view of system health.
    - ○ **Focus on uptime**: Organizations aimed to maximize availability and reduce downtime.

For instance, businesses started using threshold-based alerts that triggered warnings before a system reached a critical state, enabling teams to address issues proactively.

The Data Explosion and the Role of Big Data

The 2010s ushered in an era of unprecedented data growth, fueled by the proliferation of internet-connected devices, IoT, and cloud computing. IT operations faced new challenges in managing and analyzing this vast influx of data.

- **Key Changes**:
    - ○ **Big data technologies**: Tools like Hadoop and Spark enabled processing and analysis of large datasets.

- o **Real-time analytics**: Streaming data platforms like Kafka facilitated instant insights.
- o **Complex infrastructures**: Hybrid and multi-cloud environments required more sophisticated management.

This period also saw the rise of DevOps practices, which emphasized collaboration between development and operations teams, continuous integration, and faster delivery cycles.

The Age of Data-Driven Operations

Today, IT operations have fully embraced data-driven strategies, with Machine Learning and artificial intelligence playing pivotal roles. This evolution has shifted IT operations from being reactive to predictive and even prescriptive.

- **Key Features**:
  - o **Proactive insights**: AI-powered systems predict and prevent issues before they occur.
  - o **Anomaly detection**: Machine Learning identifies deviations from normal patterns in real-time.
  - o **Autonomous systems**: AI-driven automation handles routine tasks without human intervention.
  - o **End-to-end visibility**: Observability tools provide comprehensive insights into system performance, dependencies, and user experiences.

For example, companies use predictive analytics to forecast system load during peak times and scale resources dynamically to prevent bottlenecks, ensuring seamless user experiences.

Why Data-Driven IT Operations Matter

The evolution of IT operations reflects the growing complexity of modern systems and the critical role data plays in managing them effectively. By leveraging data and advanced analytics, organizations can:

- **Improve efficiency**: Automate routine tasks and reduce manual overhead.
- **Enhance reliability**: Identify and resolve issues before they impact users.
- **Optimize performance**: Use data insights to fine-tune systems for peak efficiency.
- **Drive innovation**: Focus on strategic initiatives rather than firefighting.

The journey from manual processes to data-driven operations underscores a fundamental truth: the ability to harness data effectively is the key to navigating the challenges of modern IT environments and achieving operational excellence.

1.2 The Importance of Data-Driven Decisions in IT Operations

In today's technology-centric world, IT operations have become the backbone of businesses across industries. These operations, responsible for ensuring the seamless functioning of infrastructure, applications, and services, are more critical and complex than ever before. To navigate this complexity effectively, organizations must adopt a data-driven approach. By leveraging the vast amounts of data generated by modern systems, IT teams can make informed decisions that improve efficiency, enhance reliability, and align operations with business objectives.

Why Data is the Foundation of Modern IT Operations

Modern IT environments generate an extraordinary amount of data. From system logs and performance metrics to user behavior and network activity, every interaction leaves a digital footprint. This wealth of information is invaluable for understanding the state of IT systems, identifying areas of improvement, and anticipating future challenges.

- **Volume and Variety**: IT systems produce data in various forms—structured (e.g. databases), semi-structured (e.g. JSON logs), and unstructured (e.g. error messages). Analyzing this data requires sophisticated tools and methodologies.
- **Real-Time Insights**: In fast-paced environments, real-time data enables immediate responses to incidents, minimizing downtime and disruption.
- **Predictive Capabilities**: Historical data allows IT teams to identify patterns and trends, making it possible to predict and prevent issues before they occur.

By tapping into this data, organizations can shift from a reactive approach to a proactive and predictive one, ensuring smooth operations and improved business outcomes.

The Challenges of Traditional Decision-Making in IT Operations

Historically, IT decisions were often made based on experience, intuition, or limited data. While this approach worked in simpler environments, it struggles to meet the demands of today's complex IT ecosystems.

- **Reactive Mindset**: Traditional IT operations focused on fixing problems after they occurred, leading to downtime and inefficiencies.
- **Limited Visibility**: Without comprehensive data, IT teams often lacked a clear understanding of system interdependencies, making troubleshooting time-consuming and error-prone.
- **Scalability Issues**: As systems expanded, manual methods of decision-making became increasingly unmanageable and prone to errors.

The limitations of this approach highlighted the need for a data-driven paradigm that could keep pace with the growing complexity of IT operations.

Benefits of Data-Driven Decision-Making in IT Operations

Adopting a data-driven approach transforms IT operations in several key ways:

1. **Improved Efficiency**:
   - Data analytics automates routine tasks such as log analysis, freeing up IT staff to focus on higher-value activities.
   - Predictive models help allocate resources efficiently, reducing wastage and improving performance.
2. **Enhanced Reliability**:
   - Real-time monitoring and anomaly detection identify potential issues before they impact users.
   - Data-driven insights enable faster root cause analysis, minimizing downtime.
3. **Proactive Problem Management**:
   - Historical data reveals patterns that can predict recurring issues, enabling proactive solutions.
   - Machine Learning models anticipate system failures, allowing preemptive maintenance.
4. **Alignment with Business Goals**:
   - Data links IT performance with business outcomes, ensuring that operations support organizational priorities.
   - Insights from data help prioritize initiatives that deliver the greatest value to the business.
5. **Scalability and Agility**:
   - Automated, data-driven processes scale seamlessly with system growth.
   - Agility improves as data empowers teams to adapt quickly to changing conditions.

Examples of Data-Driven Decisions in IT Operations

1. **Incident Prediction:**
   - A telecom company uses historical log data to predict network outages during peak usage periods, enabling pre-emptive scaling of resources.

2. **Capacity Planning:**
   - An e-commerce platform analyzes user traffic patterns to forecast resource demand during seasonal sales, ensuring seamless user experiences.

3. **Security Threat Detection:**
   - A financial institution employs anomaly detection algorithms to identify unusual login patterns, preventing potential cyberattacks.

4. **Optimized Workflows:**
   - A healthcare IT system uses real-time performance metrics to prioritize critical updates, ensuring uninterrupted access to patient records.

The Role of Machine Learning in Data-Driven IT Operations

Machine Learning amplifies the impact of data-driven decision-making by uncovering insights that are beyond human capability. These algorithms can process vast datasets, identify subtle patterns, and deliver actionable predictions in real-time.

- **Predictive Analytics**: Machine Learning models forecast future events, such as system failures or resource shortages, enabling proactive responses.
- **Anomaly Detection**: Advanced algorithms recognize deviations from normal behavior, flagging potential issues before they escalate.
- **Optimization**: ML models recommend optimal configurations and resource allocations based on historical and real-time data.

By combining human expertise with Machine Learning capabilities, IT teams can make smarter, faster, and more effective decisions.

Key Metrics for Data-Driven IT Decisions

Data-driven IT operations rely on measurable metrics to guide decision-making. Some essential metrics include:

- **Uptime and Availability**: Indicates system reliability and helps prioritize critical maintenance tasks.

- **Mean Time to Resolution (MTTR)**: Measures the efficiency of incident response and resolution.
- **Error Rates**: Highlights areas of instability within the system.
- **Resource Utilization**: Tracks how efficiently resources like CPU, memory, and storage are being used.
- **Customer Satisfaction (CSAT)**: Links IT performance with user experience, ensuring alignment with business goals.

The Strategic Advantage of Data-Driven IT Operations

Organizations that embrace data-driven decision-making gain a competitive edge in the marketplace. They can:

- **Anticipate and Prevent Disruptions**: Proactively addressing potential issues ensures uninterrupted service delivery.
- **Optimize Costs**: Efficient resource allocation and reduced downtime translate into significant cost savings.
- **Enhance Customer Experience**: Reliable systems and faster resolutions improve user satisfaction and loyalty.
- **Drive Innovation**: Data insights enable IT teams to experiment with new solutions, driving continuous improvement.

1.3 Understanding Machine Learning in IT Operations

Machine Learning (ML) has become a cornerstone of modern IT operations, fundamentally changing how organizations manage and optimize their infrastructure. In an era where data is abundant and systems are increasingly complex, Machine Learning offers the ability to uncover patterns, predict outcomes, and make intelligent decisions in real-time. This chapter introduces the concept of Machine Learning, its various types, and how it is applied to address challenges in IT operations.

What is Machine Learning?

Machine Learning is a branch of artificial intelligence that focuses on developing systems capable of learning from data and improving their performance over time without being explicitly programmed. Unlike traditional software that follows predefined rules, Machine Learning models adapt to new data, making them highly effective in dynamic environments like IT operations.

At its core, Machine Learning involves:

1. **Training**: Feeding a model with historical data to identify patterns.

2. **Validation**: Testing the model on unseen data to evaluate its accuracy.
3. **Prediction**: Using the trained model to make decisions or forecasts based on new data.

In IT operations, Machine Learning transforms how systems are monitored, maintained, and optimized, enabling proactive and efficient management.

Why Machine Learning is Crucial for IT Operations

The dynamic nature of IT operations presents unique challenges:

- **Massive Data Volumes**: Modern IT systems generate vast amounts of data, including logs, metrics, and events, making manual analysis impractical.
- **Complex Dependencies**: Applications, servers, and networks are highly interconnected, making it difficult to identify root causes of issues.
- **Real-Time Requirements**: IT operations often demand immediate responses to incidents, leaving little room for delayed decision-making.

Machine Learning addresses these challenges by:

- Automating repetitive tasks, such as log analysis.
- Identifying hidden patterns and anomalies that may not be obvious to human operators.
- Predicting system behavior to prevent outages and improve performance.

Types of Machine Learning and Their Relevance to IT Operations

Machine Learning encompasses several types, each suited to specific tasks in IT operations.

1. **Supervised Learning**:
   - **What it is**: Models are trained on labelled data, where the outcomes are known.
   - **Applications in IT**:
     - Incident classification: Categorizing issues based on historical data (e.g. "network failure" or "application error").
     - SLA breach prediction: Predicting which incidents may fail to meet service level agreements.
   - **Example**: Using a historical dataset of server failures to train a model that predicts future failures based on similar patterns.
2. **Unsupervised Learning**:
   - **What it is**: Models analyze data without predefined labels, uncovering hidden structures.
   - **Applications in IT**:

- Anomaly detection: Identifying unusual patterns in system metrics or logs.
- Clustering: Grouping similar incidents or behaviors for deeper analysis.
  - o **Example**: Detecting unusual login activities that could indicate a security breach.
3. **Reinforcement Learning**:
   - o **What it is**: Models learn by interacting with an environment and receiving feedback in the form of rewards or penalties.
   - o **Applications in IT**:
     - Resource optimization: Dynamically allocating resources to balance performance and cost.
     - Automation: Managing workflows or scaling systems based on current conditions.
   - o **Example**: Training an AI system to optimize cloud resource usage based on changing workloads.
4. **Deep Learning**:
   - o **What it is**: A subset of Machine Learning that uses neural networks to process complex, high-dimensional data.
   - o **Applications in IT**:
     - Log analysis: Extracting insights from unstructured logs.
     - Image and video processing: Analyzing visual data from surveillance systems or hardware diagnostics.
   - o **Example**: Using deep learning to parse millions of lines of log files for error patterns.

Key Machine Learning Algorithms in IT Operations
1. **Regression Models**:
   - o Used for predicting continuous variables, such as resource usage or system load.
   - o Example: Forecasting CPU utilization during peak hours.
2. **Classification Models**:
   - o Categorize data into predefined groups.
   - o Example: Identifying whether an alert is critical, warning, or informational.
3. **Clustering Algorithms**:
   - o Group similar data points together.
   - o Example: Grouping incidents with similar root causes for batch resolution.

4. **Anomaly Detection Models**:
    o   Identify data points that deviate from the norm.
    o   Example: Detecting unusual spikes in network traffic.
5. **Time Series Analysis**:
    o   Analyze temporal data to identify trends and predict future values.
    o   Example: Predicting server downtime based on historical performance metrics.

Applications of Machine Learning in IT Operations
1. **Proactive Monitoring**:
    o   ML models monitor system metrics in real-time, identifying anomalies before they escalate into major issues.
    o   Example: Detecting an unusual rise in database query latency and alerting the operations team.
2. **Incident Prediction and Prevention**:
    o   Historical data is used to predict potential incidents, enabling preventive action.
    o   Example: Predicting hardware failures based on temperature and usage trends.
3. **Automated Root Cause Analysis**:
    o   ML analyzes logs and metrics to pinpoint the root cause of system failures.
    o   Example: Automatically identifying that a memory leak caused an application crash.
4. **Capacity Planning**:
    o   Models forecast future resource needs, ensuring optimal allocation and avoiding over- or under-provisioning.
    o   Example: Predicting storage requirements during an upcoming product launch.
5. **Security Threat Detection**:
    o   ML identifies unusual patterns indicative of cyber threats.
    o   Example: Detecting multiple failed login attempts from a suspicious IP address.

Challenges in Applying Machine Learning to IT Operations
While Machine Learning offers immense potential, it also comes with challenges:
-   **Data Quality**: Incomplete or noisy data can lead to inaccurate predictions.
-   **Model Interpretability**: Complex models, like deep learning, can be difficult to interpret and trust.

- **Scalability**: ML models must handle large datasets and adapt to dynamic environments.
- **Integration**: Incorporating ML into existing IT workflows requires careful planning and alignment with organizational goals.

The Future of Machine Learning in IT Operations

The integration of Machine Learning into IT operations is still evolving, with promising advancements on the horizon:

- **AIOps (Artificial Intelligence for IT Operations)**: Combining Machine Learning, automation, and analytics to create intelligent operations systems.
- **Edge AI**: Running ML models directly on edge devices for faster decision-making.
- **Self-Healing Systems**: Systems that autonomously detect, diagnose, and resolve issues without human intervention.

These advancements point to a future where IT operations are more efficient, reliable, and adaptive than ever before.

1.4 Addressing Complex IT Challenges with Machine Learning

In the modern IT landscape, the complexity of managing infrastructures, applications, and services has grown exponentially. With distributed architectures, multi-cloud environments, and real-time user demands, traditional approaches to IT operations often fall short. Machine Learning (ML) emerges as a transformative solution to these challenges, offering intelligent, data-driven methodologies to manage, optimize, and predict IT operational outcomes. This chapter explores how Machine Learning addresses some of the most pressing and intricate IT challenges, providing scalable and proactive solutions.

The Complexity of IT Operations in the Modern Era

IT operations today face a unique blend of challenges that stem from both technological advancements and evolving user expectations:

1. **Massive Data Volumes**: IT systems generate terabytes of logs, metrics, and transactional data daily. Managing and analyzing this deluge of information manually is nearly impossible.
2. **System Interdependencies**: Modern infrastructures comprise interconnected systems, where a minor issue in one component can cascade into widespread failures.

3. **Dynamic Environments**: Cloud-native architectures, containerization, and microservices create environments that change rapidly, requiring continuous monitoring and adaptation.
4. **Real-Time Expectations**: Users demand seamless experiences, making downtime and latency unacceptable.

These complexities necessitate innovative solutions that go beyond traditional tools and practices. Machine Learning provides the intelligence needed to meet these challenges head-on.

How Machine Learning Addresses IT Challenges

Machine Learning revolutionizes IT operations by introducing automation, predictive capabilities, and advanced analytics. Below are key areas where ML excels:

1. Proactive Incident Management

Traditional IT operations often operate reactively, addressing problems only after they occur. Machine Learning enables a proactive approach, identifying potential issues before they escalate.

- **Applications**:
    - **Anomaly Detection**: Machine Learning models monitor system metrics and detect unusual patterns in real-time, flagging potential incidents.
    - **Failure Prediction**: Predictive models analyze historical data to forecast system failures or performance degradations.

Example: A cloud service provider uses ML models to predict server downtimes by analyzing temperature, CPU load, and disk usage, enabling pre-emptive maintenance.

2. Automated Root Cause Analysis

Diagnosing the root cause of incidents in complex environments can be time-consuming and error-prone. Machine Learning automates this process, reducing resolution times.

- **Applications**:
    - **Log Analysis**: Natural language processing (NLP) algorithms analyze log files to identify recurring error patterns.

- o **Dependency Mapping**: ML models map interdependencies between systems, pinpointing where failures originate.

Example: An e-commerce platform uses NLP to analyze server logs, identifying that a spike in memory usage caused a database crash.

3. Intelligent Resource Optimization
Efficient resource allocation is critical for managing costs and ensuring performance. Machine Learning models optimize resource usage by analyzing patterns and predicting future needs.

- **Applications**:
    - o **Capacity Planning**: Forecasting resource demands based on historical usage trends.
    - o **Dynamic Scaling**: Adjusting resource allocation in real-time to meet user demands.

Example: A video streaming service uses ML to predict peak traffic times and scales server capacity dynamically, ensuring uninterrupted viewing experiences.

4. Enhancing Security and Threat Detection
With the rise of sophisticated cyber threats, ensuring security has become a top priority. Machine Learning enhances threat detection by identifying unusual behaviors that may indicate breaches.

- **Applications**:
    - o **Behavioral Analytics**: Analyzing user behavior to detect anomalies, such as unusual login locations or access patterns.
    - o **Fraud Detection**: Identifying irregular transaction patterns in financial systems.

Example: A financial institution uses ML to flag suspicious transactions that deviate from a user's normal spending behavior, preventing potential fraud.

5. Real-Time Decision-Making
IT environments require instant decision-making to ensure system reliability and user satisfaction. Machine Learning models process real-time data, enabling faster responses to incidents.

- **Applications**:
  - ○ **Alert Prioritization**: Filtering out false positives and prioritizing critical alerts.
  - ○ **Adaptive Systems**: Adjusting system configurations dynamically based on current conditions.

Example: A manufacturing company uses ML to prioritize machine alerts, ensuring that critical failures are addressed immediately while low-priority issues are scheduled for later.

6. Streamlined IT Ticket Management

Managing IT tickets manually is resource-intensive and prone to delays. Machine Learning automates ticket categorization, assignment, and resolution.

- **Applications**:
  - ○ **Ticket Classification**: Using NLP to classify tickets based on descriptions.
  - ○ **Automated Resolution**: Suggesting solutions for common issues using historical ticket data.

Example: An IT service desk uses ML to categorize incoming tickets, automatically routing them to the appropriate teams and suggesting resolution steps.

7. Improved User Experience

User satisfaction is a key metric for IT operations. Machine Learning ensures optimal user experiences by predicting and resolving issues before they affect end-users.

- **Applications**:
  - ○ **Performance Optimization**: Identifying bottlenecks in application performance.
  - ○ **Personalized Services**: Using ML to adapt services based on user preferences and behavior.

Example: A telecom provider uses ML to analyze network traffic and optimize bandwidth allocation, ensuring seamless video calls for users.

The Role of Machine Learning Algorithms in Solving IT Challenges

Different Machine Learning algorithms play specific roles in addressing IT challenges:

1. **Regression Models**: Predict system loads, resource usage, and failure probabilities.
2. **Clustering Algorithms**: Group similar incidents or behaviors for bulk analysis.
3. **Decision Trees and Random Forests**: Automate classification tasks like ticket routing or alert prioritization.
4. **Deep Learning**: Process complex, high-dimensional data like logs and images for anomaly detection or diagnostics.

Each algorithm is tailored to a specific problem, ensuring accurate and actionable insights.

Overcoming Challenges with Machine Learning Adoption

While Machine Learning offers immense potential, its implementation in IT operations is not without hurdles:

1. **Data Challenges**: Ensuring the availability of clean, relevant, and labeled data for training models.
2. **Integration**: Incorporating ML models into existing workflows and tools seamlessly.
3. **Scalability**: Ensuring that models can handle the scale and velocity of IT operations data.
4. **Trust and Interpretability**: Building trust in model predictions by making them interpretable and explainable.

Organizations must address these challenges through careful planning, robust data pipelines, and continuous model validation.

1.5 Course Structure and Expected Outcomes

This book is meticulously designed to provide a comprehensive understanding of how Machine Learning can revolutionize IT operations. By focusing on real-world challenges and offering hands-on experience, this course bridges the gap between theoretical knowledge and practical application. This chapter outlines the course structure, its pedagogical approach, and the expected outcomes for learners, providing a roadmap for navigating through the journey of data-driven IT operations management.

Book Philosophy

The design of this book is rooted in three core principles:

1. **Practical Relevance**: The curriculum is tailored to address real-world IT challenges, ensuring learners acquire skills directly applicable to their professional environments.
2. **Progressive Learning**: Concepts are introduced incrementally, starting with foundational knowledge and advancing to complex topics, making it accessible to learners with varying levels of expertise.
3. **Hands-On Experience**: Emphasis is placed on practical exercises and case studies, enabling learners to apply their knowledge in simulated environments and build confidence in real-world applications.

We expect that by completing the book, learners will have a well-rounded understanding of how to harness data and Machine Learning for IT operations management, equipped with both theoretical insights and practical expertise.

Course Structure Overview

The course is structured into the following key components, each building upon the last to ensure a cohesive learning experience:

1. **Introduction to Data-Driven IT Operations**
   - **Objective**: Lay the foundation for understanding the role of data and Machine Learning in modern IT operations.
   - **Topics**: Evolution of IT operations, importance of data-driven decision-making, introduction to Machine Learning.
2. **Core Machine Learning Techniques**
   - **Objective**: Equip learners with the skills to implement Machine Learning algorithms tailored to IT operations.
   - **Topics**: Supervised and unsupervised learning, anomaly detection, time series analysis, and NLP.
3. **Real-World Case Studies**
   - **Objective**: Explore practical applications of Machine Learning in solving IT challenges.
   - **Topics**: Predictive maintenance, resource optimization, ticket classification, and root cause analysis.
4. **Capstone Project**
   - **Objective**: Provide a holistic platform for learners to apply their skills in a comprehensive, real-world scenario.
   - **Topics**: End-to-end solution design for IT operations challenges using Machine Learning.

Each component is designed to balance theoretical concepts with practical implementation, ensuring that learners can immediately apply what they learn.

Detailed Breakdown of the Chapters

Each chapter in this book is dedicated to solving a specific IT challenge using Machine Learning. The chapters include:

1. **Predicting System Downtime**
   o **Objective**: Teach learners how to use time series forecasting to predict potential downtimes.
   o **Outcome**: Learners will create predictive models that enable proactive system maintenance.
2. **Real-Time Anomaly Detection**
   o **Objective**: Implement anomaly detection models to identify unusual patterns in system behavior.
   o **Outcome**: Enhanced real-time monitoring capabilities.
3. **Automating Root Cause Analysis**
   o **Objective**: Use log analysis and NLP to pinpoint the root causes of IT issues.
   o **Outcome**: Faster incident resolution and reduced downtime.
4. **Optimizing Resource Allocation**
   o **Objective**: Apply regression techniques to optimize the allocation of IT resources.
   o **Outcome**: Cost savings and improved system performance.
5. **Incident Categorization and Ticket Routing**
   o **Objective**: Automate incident categorization using Machine Learning.
   o **Outcome**: Streamlined ticket management and faster issue resolution.

Learning Methodology

The book employs a blend of instructional methods to ensure a rich and engaging learning experience:

1. **Conceptual Lectures**: Provide theoretical grounding in Machine Learning and IT operations concepts.
2. **Hands-On Exercises**: Offer opportunities to work with real-world datasets, applying Machine Learning algorithms to solve IT challenges.
3. **Case Studies**: Demonstrate practical applications of the techniques discussed, contextualizing them within real IT operations scenarios.

4. **Capstone Project**: Allow learners to integrate their knowledge and skills into a comprehensive, end-to-end project.

Expected Outcomes

By reading this book and practicing the examples given here, learners will:

1. **Develop Technical Expertise**:
    o   Understand the role of Machine Learning in IT operations.
    o   Gain proficiency in implementing Machine Learning algorithms to solve IT challenges.
2. **Enhance Problem-Solving Skills**:
    o   Identify IT challenges suitable for Machine Learning applications.
    o   Analyze large datasets and derive actionable insights to improve IT operations.
3. **Apply Real-World Solutions**:
    o   Design and implement Machine Learning models for tasks like anomaly detection, predictive maintenance, and resource optimization.
    o   Use Machine Learning to streamline processes like ticket management and root cause analysis.
4. **Build a Portfolio of Work**:
    o   Develop a portfolio of projects demonstrating the application of Machine Learning in IT operations.
    o   Gain hands-on experience with tools and technologies used in the industry.
5. **Drive Organizational Impact**:
    o   Transition from reactive to proactive IT management strategies.
    o   Align IT operations with broader business objectives through data-driven decision-making.

The course structure is meticulously designed to ensure learners gain a deep understanding of how data and Machine Learning can transform IT operations. By progressing through these chapters, learners will acquire not only the theoretical knowledge but also the practical skills required to address complex IT challenges with confidence. This comprehensive approach ensures that learners are prepared to excel in real-world environments, making them valuable contributors to their organizations and leaders in the evolving landscape of IT operations.

1.6 Setting Expectations for Learners

Embarking on a journey to master data-driven IT operations using Machine Learning is both exciting and demanding. This chapter sets clear expectations for learners, outlining the skills, mindset, and tools required to succeed in the course. By understanding these expectations upfront, learners can prepare themselves effectively, ensuring a more enriching and fulfilling learning experience.

Who Is This Course For?

This course is designed for a diverse audience with varying levels of experience in IT and data analysis. It is tailored to meet the needs of the following groups:

1. **IT Professionals**:
   - System administrators, IT operations managers, and infrastructure engineers who aim to integrate Machine Learning into their workflows to enhance efficiency and reliability.
2. **Data Analysts**:
   - Professionals with experience in analyzing data who wish to apply their skills to IT operations and develop predictive and prescriptive analytics capabilities.
3. **Machine Learning Enthusiasts**:
   - Individuals with a basic understanding of Machine Learning who want to explore its applications in IT operations management.
4. **Business and Technical Leaders**:
   - Decision-makers seeking to understand how data-driven strategies can transform IT operations and align with organizational goals.

This course assumes that learners bring curiosity, a willingness to explore, and an eagerness to solve real-world problems, regardless of their professional backgrounds.

What Skills Do Learners Need?

While the course is designed to be accessible, certain foundational skills will help learners make the most of the material. These include:

1. **Basic IT Operations Knowledge**:
   - Familiarity with IT infrastructure, such as servers, networks, and databases.
   - An understanding of common IT challenges like downtime, incident management, and capacity planning.

2. **Data Analysis Fundamentals**:
    - o Basic proficiency in handling and analyzing data using tools like Excel, SQL, or Python.
    - o An understanding of key data concepts such as trends, patterns, and anomalies.
3. **Programming Basics**:
    - o Familiarity with Python is highly beneficial, as it will be used for implementing Machine Learning models.
    - o Experience with libraries like Pandas, NumPy, and Scikit-learn can provide a head start.
4. **Problem-Solving Mindset**:
    - o A logical approach to breaking down complex problems into manageable components.
    - o A willingness to experiment, iterate, and learn from failures.

Tools and Resources Required

Learners will use a combination of software tools and datasets to complete exercises and projects throughout the course. These include:

1. **Software and Platforms**:
    - o **Python**: The primary programming language for implementing Machine Learning algorithms.
    - o **Jupyter Notebooks**: For writing and testing code interactively.
    - o **Machine Learning Libraries**: Scikit-learn, TensorFlow, or PyTorch for building and training models.
    - o **Data Visualization Tools**: Matplotlib and Seaborn for creating visual insights.
2. **Datasets**:
    - o Real-world datasets related to IT operations, such as system logs, performance metrics, and incident tickets, will be provided.
    - o Learners are encouraged to explore open-source datasets to supplement their learning.
3. **Cloud Platforms (Optional)**:
    - o Platforms like AWS, Azure, or Google Cloud can be used for deploying Machine Learning solutions in a real-world environment.

Mindset and Approach for Success

To maximize the value of this course, learners are encouraged to adopt the following attitudes and practices:

1. **Curiosity and Exploration**:
   - Be open to exploring new concepts and technologies. Machine Learning is a dynamic field, and a willingness to learn continuously is essential.
2. **Hands-On Learning**:
   - Actively engage with the exercises, case studies, and projects. Practical application is key to mastering the concepts.
3. **Collaboration and Discussion**:
   - Participate in discussions with peers, ask questions, and share insights. Learning collaboratively can deepen understanding.
4. **Embrace Challenges**:
   - Some concepts and exercises may be challenging, especially for those new to Machine Learning. Persistence and resilience are crucial to overcoming these hurdles.
5. **Focus on Real-World Applications**:
   - Think critically about how the skills learned can be applied to your own organization or professional context. This will make the learning experience more relevant and impactful.

What Learners Will Gain from the Book

By setting clear expectations, learners can visualize the value this course will add to their professional skillset. The outcomes include:

1. **Comprehensive Knowledge**:
   - A deep understanding of how Machine Learning can transform IT operations and solve complex challenges.
2. **Practical Skills**:
   - Hands-on experience in applying Machine Learning algorithms to real-world IT datasets and scenarios.
3. **Problem-Solving Confidence**:
   - The ability to identify, analyze, and address IT challenges using data-driven strategies.
4. **Career Advancement**:
   - Enhanced skills that are highly valued in roles such as IT Operations Analyst, Data Scientist, or AI Specialist.
5. **Portfolio of Work**:
   - A collection of projects showcasing your ability to apply Machine Learning in IT operations, which can be used to demonstrate expertise to employers or clients.

Setting clear expectations is crucial for ensuring that learners are prepared to succeed in this course. By understanding the required skills, tools, and mindset, learners can approach the material with confidence and clarity. This chapter serves as a roadmap, helping learners align their goals with the course objectives and paving the way for a transformative learning experience. With the right preparation and attitude, participants will not only master data-driven IT operations but also position themselves as leaders in this rapidly evolving field.

1.7 The Road Ahead: Embracing Data-Driven IT Operations

The future of IT operations lies firmly in the realm of data-driven strategies and intelligent automation. As organizations increasingly rely on technology to support business functions, the complexity of IT systems and the volume of data they generate continue to grow exponentially. This chapter explores the trajectory of IT operations as they evolve into more proactive, predictive, and self-sustaining systems through the use of data and Machine Learning. It highlights the opportunities, challenges, and innovations that lie ahead and emphasizes the importance of adopting a forward-thinking mindset to navigate this transformation effectively.

The Shifting Paradigm in IT Operations

Traditional IT operations, characterized by manual processes and reactive problem-solving, are no longer sufficient to meet the demands of modern organizations. The rapid evolution of technology, combined with the need for 24/7 availability and seamless user experiences, has necessitated a shift toward more data-driven and intelligent systems.

1. **From Reactive to Proactive**:
   - In the past, IT teams primarily addressed issues after they occurred, often resulting in downtime and lost productivity.
   - Today, data-driven insights enable proactive monitoring and maintenance, allowing potential issues to be identified and resolved before they escalate.
2. **From Manual to Automated**:
   - Manual processes are being replaced by intelligent automation powered by Machine Learning. Tasks such as log analysis, resource allocation, and ticket routing are now handled autonomously, freeing up IT staff for strategic initiatives.

3. **From Isolated to Integrated**:
   - Modern IT operations integrate data from diverse sources, providing a holistic view of the IT ecosystem. This integration enhances decision-making and ensures that systems operate in harmony.

Opportunities in Data-Driven IT Operations

As IT operations become more data-centric, organizations can unlock a host of opportunities that drive efficiency, innovation, and competitive advantage:

1. **Enhanced Decision-Making**:
   - Data analytics and Machine Learning models provide actionable insights, enabling IT teams to make informed decisions quickly and accurately.
   - For example, predictive analytics can forecast resource needs, ensuring optimal allocation and preventing capacity issues.
2. **Improved User Experience**:
   - By analyzing user behavior and system performance, organizations can identify and address pain points, delivering a seamless and satisfying user experience.
   - For instance, real-time monitoring of application performance can detect and resolve latency issues before users are impacted.
3. **Cost Optimization**:
   - Intelligent resource management minimizes waste and reduces operational costs. Machine Learning models can identify underutilized resources and recommend adjustments to improve efficiency.
   - For example, dynamic scaling ensures that cloud resources are only used when needed, avoiding unnecessary expenses.
4. **Innovation and Agility**:
   - Data-driven IT operations empower organizations to experiment with new technologies and processes, fostering a culture of innovation.
   - Agile methodologies supported by data insights enable faster adaptation to changing business needs and technological advancements.

Challenges on the Road Ahead

While the potential of data-driven IT operations is immense, organizations must address several challenges to fully realize its benefits:

1. **Data Management**:
   - The sheer volume and variety of data generated by IT systems can be overwhelming. Ensuring data quality, consistency, and accessibility is crucial for effective analysis.
   - Organizations must invest in robust data pipelines, storage solutions, and governance frameworks.

2. **Skill Gaps**:
   - Implementing data-driven strategies requires a skilled workforce with expertise in data analytics, Machine Learning, and IT operations.
   - Continuous training and upskilling programs are essential to bridge this gap and empower IT teams.

3. **Integration Complexity**:
   - Integrating Machine Learning models into existing IT workflows and tools can be challenging, particularly in legacy systems.
   - Collaboration between data scientists, IT professionals, and business stakeholders is critical to ensure seamless integration.

4. **Trust and Transparency**:
   - Building trust in Machine Learning models and their predictions is vital. Models must be interpretable, and their decision-making processes should be transparent.
   - Ethical considerations, such as avoiding bias and ensuring data privacy, must also be addressed.

The Role of Emerging Technologies

Several emerging technologies are shaping the future of data-driven IT operations, offering new possibilities for innovation and efficiency:

1. **AIOps (Artificial Intelligence for IT Operations)**:
   - AIOps platforms combine Machine Learning, big data, and automation to provide intelligent insights and recommendations for IT operations.
   - These platforms enable real-time anomaly detection, root cause analysis, and predictive maintenance, reducing downtime and improving reliability.

2. **Edge Computing**:
   - As IoT devices proliferate, edge computing allows data processing to occur closer to the source, reducing latency and enabling real-time decision-making.
   - For example, edge AI can monitor and control industrial equipment in real-time, enhancing operational efficiency.

3. **Self-Healing Systems**:
   - Self-healing systems use Machine Learning to autonomously detect, diagnose, and resolve issues without human intervention.
   - These systems reduce the need for manual troubleshooting and improve system resilience.

4. **Cloud-Native Architectures**:
   - Cloud-native technologies, such as containers and serverless computing, provide the scalability and flexibility needed for data-driven IT operations.
   - Machine Learning models can dynamically adapt to changing workloads in cloud environments, ensuring optimal performance.

Key Principles for Embracing Data-Driven IT Operations

To successfully transition to data-driven IT operations, organizations should adopt the following principles:

1. **Invest in Infrastructure**:
   - Build robust data pipelines, storage solutions, and analytics platforms to support data-driven decision-making.
   - Ensure scalability and flexibility to accommodate future growth and technological advancements.

2. **Foster a Culture of Collaboration**:
   - Encourage collaboration between IT teams, data scientists, and business leaders to align technical solutions with organizational goals.
   - Create cross-functional teams that can leverage diverse expertise to solve complex challenges.

3. **Prioritize Continuous Learning**:
   - Establish training programs to upskill employees in data analytics, Machine Learning, and IT operations.
   - Stay updated on emerging technologies and industry trends to remain competitive.

4. **Focus on Ethics and Governance**:
   - o Implement policies to ensure data privacy, security, and compliance with regulatory requirements.
   - o Address ethical considerations, such as fairness and transparency, in Machine Learning applications.

The Vision for the Future

The road ahead for data-driven IT operations is one of continuous evolution and innovation. Organizations that embrace this transformation will enjoy a competitive edge, leveraging data and Machine Learning to create more efficient, reliable, and agile IT environments. By addressing challenges proactively and adopting emerging technologies, IT operations can become a strategic enabler of business success.

As we move into the subsequent chapters, this course will delve deeper into specific applications of data-driven IT operations, exploring how Machine Learning can solve real-world challenges and drive tangible outcomes. By the end of this journey, learners will be equipped with the knowledge and skills to shape the future of IT operations in their organizations and beyond.

* * *

Predicting System Downtime
Using Historical Logs

CHAPTER 2

PREDICTING SYSTEM DOWNTIME USING HISTORICAL LOGS

This chapter introduces learners to using historical log data and Machine Learning techniques to predict system downtime. By leveraging time-series forecasting algorithms, participants will develop models to anticipate potential outages, enabling proactive maintenance and enhancing system reliability.

2.1 Introduction to Predictive Maintenance in IT Operations

Predictive maintenance has emerged as a transformative approach in IT operations, offering a proactive way to manage systems, ensure uptime, and prevent costly disruptions. In this section, we delve into the concept of predictive maintenance, its significance in modern IT environments, and the foundational role of historical log data in achieving its objectives.

What is Predictive Maintenance?

Predictive maintenance refers to the practice of using data-driven techniques and advanced analytics to anticipate when a system or component is likely to fail. Unlike traditional maintenance strategies, which are either reactive (addressing issues after they occur) or scheduled (conducting maintenance at fixed intervals), predictive maintenance focuses on real-time monitoring and forecasting to prevent failures before they happen.

- **Reactive Maintenance:**
  - Addressing problems only after they occur, leading to downtime and often higher repair costs.
  - Example: Replacing a server only after it crashes, resulting in service interruptions.
- **Scheduled Maintenance:**
  - Performing maintenance at regular intervals, regardless of the actual condition of the system.
  - Example: Monthly checks of all servers, even those operating perfectly, leading to unnecessary costs or overlooked issues.

- **Predictive Maintenance**:
  - o Monitoring the condition of systems continuously and predicting failures based on data patterns.
  - o Example: Using system logs and performance metrics to predict that a server's CPU will fail within the next 48 hours.

By transitioning to predictive maintenance, IT operations can become more proactive, optimizing resource utilization and minimizing unexpected disruptions.

Significance of Predictive Maintenance in IT Operations

The complexity of modern IT infrastructures has increased significantly, with organizations relying on cloud environments, distributed systems, and microservices to power their operations. This shift has introduced several challenges, including:

1. **High Stakes for Downtime**:
   - o System failures can lead to lost revenue, damaged reputations, and diminished customer trust.
   - o Example: An e-commerce platform experiencing an unplanned outage during a sales event.
2. **Escalating Maintenance Costs**:
   - o Reactive and scheduled maintenance often result in inefficient use of resources.
   - o Predictive maintenance optimizes maintenance schedules, reducing costs while ensuring reliability.
3. **Data Explosion**:
   - o IT systems generate massive amounts of log data daily, making manual analysis impractical.
   - o Predictive maintenance leverages this data to derive actionable insights.
4. **Real-Time User Demands**:
   - o With users expecting seamless experiences, even minor disruptions can lead to dissatisfaction.
   - o Example: Delayed responses in a banking app due to server performance issues.

How Predictive Maintenance Works in IT Operations

Predictive maintenance relies on a combination of historical data, real-time monitoring, and advanced analytics to anticipate potential failures. The key steps include:

1. **Data Collection**:
   - ○ Gathering data from various sources, such as system logs, application performance metrics, and hardware sensors.
   - ○ Example: Logs capturing CPU usage, memory consumption, and disk I/O rates.
2. **Data Analysis**:
   - ○ Using Machine Learning algorithms to analyze historical patterns and identify trends that precede failures.
   - ○ Example: Analyzing CPU temperature spikes that often occur before a server crashes.
3. **Failure Prediction**:
   - ○ Generating forecasts about when and where failures are likely to occur.
   - ○ Example: Predicting that a database server will experience high memory utilization within the next 24 hours, leading to a potential failure.
4. **Proactive Action**:
   - ○ Scheduling maintenance activities or deploying fixes based on predictions.
   - ○ Example: Replacing a failing hard drive before it leads to system downtime.

The Role of Historical Log Data in Predictive Maintenance

Historical log data serves as the backbone of predictive maintenance in IT operations. Logs capture a detailed account of system activities, errors, and performance metrics, providing invaluable insights into system behavior over time.

- **Key Components of Log Data**:
  1. **Timestamps**: Record the exact time of events, enabling time-series analysis.
  2. **Error Codes**: Indicate specific issues or anomalies within the system.
  3. **Performance Metrics**: Track CPU usage, memory consumption, and disk I/O rates, reflecting system health.

- **How Logs Contribute to Predictive Maintenance**:
  - ○ Detecting anomalies: Logs help identify deviations from normal patterns, such as unexpected spikes in resource utilization.

- o Correlating events: Logs provide context for understanding how one event might lead to another, such as a disk I/O bottleneck causing a database timeout.
- o Training predictive models: Historical logs are used to train Machine Learning models to predict future failures with high accuracy.

Benefits of Predictive Maintenance in IT Operations
1. **Minimized Downtime**:
    - o By predicting and addressing issues before they occur, predictive maintenance significantly reduces unplanned outages.
2. **Cost Efficiency**:
    - o Optimizes resource utilization, avoiding unnecessary maintenance while preventing costly failures.
3. **Enhanced Reliability**:
    - o Ensures that systems operate smoothly, improving user satisfaction and trust.
4. **Data-Driven Decision Making**:
    - o Provides IT teams with actionable insights, empowering them to make informed decisions.

Predictive maintenance represents a paradigm shift in IT operations, moving from reactive and manual processes to proactive and intelligent systems. By leveraging historical log data and advanced analytics, organizations can anticipate and mitigate potential issues, ensuring higher uptime, reduced costs, and improved system reliability. As we proceed, this chapter sets the stage for implementing predictive maintenance using Machine Learning algorithms and real-world log data, equipping learners with the tools to transform IT operations into a proactive powerhouse.

2.2 Preparing Data for Predictive Modelling

The success of predictive modelling in IT operations heavily relies on the quality and relevance of the data being used. Preparing data for predictive maintenance involves collecting, cleaning, transforming, and engineering features from raw data to make it suitable for Machine Learning algorithms. This section dives deep into the processes and best practices for preparing historical log data, enabling accurate and actionable predictions for system downtime.

1. Data Collection and Sources

Predictive modelling begins with collecting the right data from reliable sources. In IT operations, data is often generated continuously from various systems, applications, and hardware components. These data sources include:

1. **System Logs**:
    - Generated by operating systems to track events such as resource usage, errors, and warnings.
    - Example: Logs showing CPU utilization spikes or memory errors.
2. **Application Logs**:
    - Captures information about application performance, errors, and user interactions.
    - Example: Logs tracking HTTP response times and API errors in a web application.
3. **Infrastructure Monitoring Tools**:
    - Tools like Prometheus, Nagios, or Splunk provide real-time monitoring data for system performance.
    - Example: Data showing server temperatures or disk I/O rates.
4. **Hardware Sensors**:
    - Sensors embedded in hardware components (e.g. CPUs, hard drives) provide metrics like temperature, fan speed, and power consumption.
    - Example: SMART (Self-Monitoring, Analysis, and Reporting Technology) data for hard drives.

Best Practices for Data Collection:

- Ensure data is collected at consistent intervals to capture trends over time.
- Centralize logs using tools like ELK Stack (Elasticsearch, Logstash, Kibana) or Splunk for easier analysis.
- Retain historical data for extended periods to identify long-term patterns and trends.

2. Data Cleaning and Preprocessing

Raw log data is often noisy, incomplete, or inconsistent, making cleaning and preprocessing critical steps before analysis. Key tasks include:

1. **Handling Missing Data**:
    - Identify missing values in critical metrics like CPU usage or memory utilization.

- o Strategies:
  - ▪ **Imputation**: Replace missing values with mean, median, or forward-fill values.
  - ▪ **Removal**: Discard records with excessive missing data if imputation is not feasible.
2. **Removing Duplicates**:
   - o Ensure that duplicate log entries are removed to avoid over-representation of specific events.
3. **Filtering Irrelevant Records**:
   - o Exclude logs unrelated to system health or performance, such as debug or informational logs.
4. **Normalization and Scaling**:
   - o Normalize metrics like CPU usage or memory utilization to a consistent scale (e.g. 0–1) to avoid bias in model training.
   - o Example: Normalized Value = (Value–Min) / (Max–Min)
5. **Time Alignment**:
   - o Ensure that logs from different sources are aligned by timestamp to facilitate correlation analysis.

3. Feature Engineering

Feature engineering transforms raw data into meaningful inputs for predictive models. This step is crucial for improving model performance and interpretability.

1. **Creating Rolling Statistics**:
   - o Compute rolling averages, maximums, or standard deviations for metrics over time.
   - o Example: A rolling average of CPU usage over the last 6 hours to detect abnormal spikes.
2. **Lag Features**:
   - o Introduce lagged versions of metrics to capture temporal dependencies.
   - o Example: Adding a column for CPU usage from 1 hour prior.
3. **Error Count Trends**:
   - o Track the frequency of error codes over specific time intervals.
   - o Example: Count the occurrences of error code E001 in the past 24 hours.
4. **Event Flags**:
   - o Create binary features indicating the presence of critical events, such as high memory usage or specific error codes.

5. **Anomaly Scores**:
   - o Use unsupervised learning techniques to generate anomaly scores for each record.
   - o Example: Use k-means clustering to label unusual disk I/O patterns as anomalies.

4. Aggregating and Resampling Data

Log data is often recorded at granular levels, such as seconds or milliseconds. Aggregating and resampling this data into meaningful intervals simplifies analysis while preserving key trends.

1. **Choosing an Interval**:
   - o Determine the appropriate time interval for aggregation based on the use case.
   - o Example: Aggregate logs into hourly intervals for predicting downtime over the next 24 hours.
2. **Aggregation Functions**:
   - o Apply aggregation functions to summarize data within each interval.
   - o Common functions: Mean, sum, maximum, minimum, and standard deviation.
   - o Example: Calculate the average CPU usage and maximum memory usage for each hour.
3. **Event Resampling**:
   - o Consolidate event logs into time buckets, counting the number of occurrences within each bucket.
   - o Example: Count the number of disks read errors per hour.

5. Data Validation

Before proceeding to model building, it's essential to validate the cleaned and processed data to ensure it aligns with the intended analysis goals.

1. **Check for Completeness**:
   - o Verify that all required metrics and features are present for each time interval.
2. **Detect Outliers**:
   - o Use statistical methods (e.g. z-scores, IQR) to identify and handle outliers in metrics.
3. **Visualize Data**:
   - o Plot key metrics over time to identify trends, seasonality, and anomalies.

- o Example: Visualize CPU usage over the past week to detect recurring patterns.

6. Tools and Libraries for Data Preparation
Several tools and libraries can simplify data preparation tasks:

1. **Python Libraries**:
   - o **Pandas**: Data cleaning, aggregation, and resampling.
   - o **NumPy**: Mathematical operations for feature engineering.
   - o **Scikit-learn**: Preprocessing and feature transformation.
2. **Log Aggregation Tools**:
   - o **Splunk**: Real-time log monitoring and analysis.
   - o **ELK Stack**: Open-source suite for log collection and visualization.
3. **Visualization Tools**:
   - o **Matplotlib** and **Seaborn**: For creating time-series plots and anomaly visualizations.

7. Practical Example: Preparing a Synthetic Dataset
Let's consider a synthetic dataset with the following schema:
- **Timestamp**: YYYY-MM-DD HH:MM:SS
- **Error_Code**: E001, E002, ...
- **CPU_Usage**: Percentage values (0–100).
- **Memory_Usage**: Percentage values (0–100).
- **Disk_IO_Rate**: Disk read/write rate (0–500).
- **Uptime_Status**: Binary (1 = system up, 0 = system down).

Steps:
1. Load the synthetic dataset into a Pandas DataFrame.
2. Clean missing and duplicate records.
3. Engineer lag features, rolling statistics, and event flags.
4. Aggregate data into hourly intervals.
5. Validate the processed dataset using visualizations.

Data preparation is a critical foundation for predictive modelling in IT operations. Properly cleaned and engineered data ensures that Machine Learning models receive accurate and meaningful inputs, enhancing their predictive power. By mastering these techniques, learners can transform raw log data into actionable insights, setting the stage for building robust downtime prediction models in the next section.

2.3 Understanding Time-Series Forecasting

Time-series forecasting is a critical component of predictive analytics, especially in the realm of IT operations, where historical data trends often hold the key to anticipating future outcomes. In this section, we delve into the foundational concepts of time-series forecasting, its unique characteristics, and its significance in predicting system downtimes. By understanding the nuances of time-series data, learners can leverage this powerful technique to create models that provide actionable insights for proactive IT operations management.

What is Time-Series Forecasting?

Time-series forecasting is the process of analyzing temporal data to predict future values based on historical patterns. Unlike traditional datasets where observations are independent, time-series data has a sequential nature, with each data point being dependent on the previous ones.

In the context of IT operations, time-series forecasting can predict metrics like:

- CPU usage spikes.
- Memory utilization trends.
- Disk I/O bottlenecks.
- Likelihood of system downtime.

This ability to anticipate future events empowers organizations to take proactive actions, such as scaling resources, scheduling maintenance, or preventing system failures.

Characteristics of Time-Series Data

Understanding the unique attributes of time-series data is essential for effective forecasting. Key characteristics include:

1. **Temporal Dependency**:
   - Time-series data is inherently sequential, with each observation dependent on its predecessors.
   - Example: A sudden increase in CPU usage at 10 AM is likely influenced by system activity at 9:30 AM.

2. **Seasonality**:
   - Repeating patterns or cycles in data occurring at regular intervals.
   - Example: Increased server traffic during peak business hours or weekends.

3. **Trends**:
   - Long-term upward or downward movement in data.
   - Example: Gradual growth in memory usage due to expanding application demands.

4. **Noise**:
   - ○ Random variations in data that do not follow any specific pattern.
   - ○ Example: Sudden, unexplained spikes in disk I/O rates.
5. **Stationarity**:
   - ○ A stationary time series has constant mean and variance over time.
   - ○ Non-stationary data often requires transformation (e.g. differencing) before modeling.

Why Use Time-Series Forecasting in IT Operations?

Time-series forecasting provides IT teams with a structured approach to predicting critical metrics and events, enabling more efficient and reliable operations. Key benefits include:

1. **Proactive Maintenance**:
   - ○ Predict hardware or software failures before they occur, minimizing downtime.
   - ○ Example: Forecasting disk usage to ensure storage upgrades are scheduled in advance.
2. **Resource Optimization**:
   - ○ Anticipate resource demands and allocate capacity effectively.
   - ○ Example: Scaling cloud resources during anticipated traffic surges.
3. **Enhanced User Experience**:
   - ○ Avoid service disruptions by proactively addressing potential performance bottlenecks.
   - ○ Example: Predicting and preventing server overload during high-traffic events.
4. **Cost Efficiency**:
   - ○ Reduce unnecessary expenditures by accurately forecasting resource requirements.
   - ○ Example: Preventing over-provisioning in data centers.

Approaches to Time-Series Forecasting

There are several methods to forecast time-series data, ranging from classical statistical models to advanced Machine Learning and deep learning techniques. Let's explore these approaches:

1. **Classical Statistical Models**:
   - ○ These models assume linear relationships in the data and are suitable for small to moderate datasets.
   - ○ Examples:
     - ▪ **ARIMA (Autoregressive Integrated Moving Average)**:

- Combines autoregression, differencing, and moving averages to model trends and seasonality.
  - **Exponential Smoothing**:
    - Assigns exponentially decreasing weights to older observations, focusing on recent data.

2. **Machine Learning Models**:
   - These models can capture non-linear patterns and interactions in the data.
   - Examples:
     - **Random Forest Regressor**:
       - Uses decision trees to predict future values.
     - **Gradient Boosting Machines (e.g. XGBoost, LightGBM)**:
       - Powerful algorithms for handling complex time-series relationships.
3. **Deep Learning Models**:
   - Suitable for large and complex datasets with intricate temporal dependencies.
   - Examples:
     - **LSTM (Long Short-Term Memory)**:
       - A type of recurrent neural network (RNN) designed to handle long-term dependencies in sequential data.
     - **GRU (Gated Recurrent Unit)**:
       - Similar to LSTM but with fewer parameters, making it computationally efficient.
4. **Hybrid Models**:
   - Combine statistical models with Machine Learning to leverage the strengths of both approaches.
   - Example: Using ARIMA for trend modeling and LSTM for capturing non-linear dependencies.

Steps in Time-Series Forecasting

The process of time-series forecasting involves several key steps:

1. **Exploratory Data Analysis (EDA)**:
   - Visualize the time-series data to identify trends, seasonality, and anomalies.
   - Example: Plot CPU usage over time to detect recurring patterns.
2. **Data Preprocessing**:
   - Handle missing values, outliers, and noise.

o   Transform non-stationary data to make it suitable for modeling.

3. **Feature Engineering**:
   o   Create lag features, rolling statistics, and time-based attributes.
   o   Example: Adding a "day of the week" feature to account for weekly seasonality.

4. **Model Selection**:
   o   Choose an appropriate forecasting model based on data characteristics and project goals.

5. **Model Training and Validation**:
   o   Train the model using historical data and evaluate its performance using metrics like RMSE (Root Mean Square Error) or MAPE (Mean Absolute Percentage Error).

6. **Forecasting and Deployment**:
   o   Generate predictions and integrate them into IT workflows for real-time decision-making.

Evaluating Forecasting Performance

Accurate forecasting is critical to the success of predictive maintenance. Performance evaluation ensures that the model reliably predicts future events. Common evaluation metrics include:

1. **RMSE (Root Mean Square Error)**:
   o   Measures the average magnitude of prediction errors.
   o   Lower values indicate better performance.

2. **MAPE (Mean Absolute Percentage Error)**:
   o   Measures error as a percentage of actual values, making it interpretable.
   o   Ideal for comparing models across different datasets.

3. **Cross-Validation**:
   o   Splitting data into training and testing sets based on time periods to validate model accuracy.

Example Application in IT Operations

Consider a server monitoring system generating hourly logs of CPU usage, memory utilization, and error counts. Using time-series forecasting, an IT team can:

1. Identify patterns in CPU spikes during peak hours.
2. Predict when memory usage will exceed critical thresholds.
3. Schedule resource scaling or maintenance to prevent downtime.

For instance, an LSTM model trained on historical CPU usage data can predict a 90% utilization spike in the next 12 hours, prompting proactive action.

Challenges in Time-Series Forecasting
While powerful, time-series forecasting is not without challenges:
1. **Data Quality Issues**:
   o Missing or noisy data can lead to inaccurate predictions.
2. **Overfitting**:
   o Complex models like LSTM can overfit the training data, reducing generalizability.
3. **External Factors**:
   o Unexpected events (e.g. cyberattacks, hardware failures) may disrupt patterns, impacting model accuracy.

Time-series forecasting is a cornerstone of predictive maintenance in IT operations. By understanding its characteristics, methodologies, and applications, IT teams can anticipate system behavior, optimize resources, and enhance reliability. In the next section, we will apply these concepts to real-world data, building models to predict system downtime and unlock actionable insights.

2.4 Implementing Time-Series Forecasting for Downtime Prediction

Problem Statement
System downtime in IT operations is costly and disruptive. Predicting downtime using historical log data allows proactive maintenance and reduces unexpected failures. The goal is to implement a time-series forecasting model using the ARIMA (Autoregressive Integrated Moving Average) method to predict system performance metrics and anticipate downtime.

Steps to Solve the Problem
Step 1: Data Preparation
   - Load historical log data.
   - Resample the data into hourly intervals for consistency.
   - Handle missing values by filling them with the mean of the respective metric.

Step 2: Exploratory Data Analysis
   - Visualize the time-series data to identify trends, seasonality, and noise.

Step 3: ARIMA Model Implementation
- Fit the ARIMA model to the training dataset.
- Use the model to forecast system performance on the test dataset.

Step 4: Evaluation
- Calculate Root Mean Squared Error (RMSE) to evaluate forecast accuracy.
- Visualize the actual vs. predicted values to understand model performance.

Step 5: Deployment and Insights
- Save the results and integrate the model into the IT workflow to provide actionable insights for proactive decision-making.

Python Code Implementation

```python
import pandas as pd
import numpy as np
from statsmodels.tsa.arima.model import ARIMA
import matplotlib.pyplot as plt
from sklearn.metrics import mean_squared_error

# Load the synthetic dataset
file_path = "log_data.csv"  # Ensure this file is available in your
working directory
log_data = pd.read_csv(file_path, parse_dates=["Timestamp"],
index_col="Timestamp")

# Filter data for the relevant metric (e.g. CPU Usage)
log_data = log_data.resample('H').mean()  # Resample to hourly
intervals
cpu_usage = log_data['CPU_Usage']

# Check for missing values and handle them
cpu_usage = cpu_usage.fillna(cpu_usage.mean())

# Ensure non-numeric columns are excluded (if present)
if not np.issubdtype(cpu_usage.dtype, np.number):
    raise ValueError("The selected column contains non-numeric
data.")

# Split data into training and testing sets
train_size = int(len(cpu_usage) * 0.8)
train, test = cpu_usage[:train_size], cpu_usage[train_size:]

# Fit the ARIMA model
```

```python
model = ARIMA(train, order=(5, 1, 0))  # Order: p=5, d=1, q=0
model_fit = model.fit()

# Forecast
forecast = model_fit.forecast(steps=len(test))

# Calculate and print evaluation metrics
rmse = np.sqrt(mean_squared_error(test, forecast))
print(f"Root Mean Squared Error (RMSE): {rmse}")

# Plot the results
plt.figure(figsize=(12, 6))
plt.plot(train, label="Training Data")
plt.plot(test, label="Test Data")
plt.plot(test.index, forecast, label="Forecast", color='red')
plt.title("CPU Usage Forecasting with ARIMA")
plt.xlabel("Time")
plt.ylabel("CPU Usage (%)")
plt.legend()
plt.grid()
plt.show()

# Save the model and predictions (optional)
forecast_df = pd.DataFrame({"Actual": test, "Forecast": forecast},
index=test.index)
forecast_df.to_csv("cpu_usage_forecast_results_arima.csv")

print("Forecasting complete. Results saved to
'cpu_usage_forecast_results_arima.csv'.")
```

Code Explanation

1. Data Preparation:
   - The dataset is loaded and resampled into hourly intervals.
   - Missing values are filled with the mean of the CPU usage metric.

2. ARIMA Model Fitting:
   - The ARIMA model is configured with order (5, 1, 0), which includes 5 autoregressive terms, 1 differencing term, and no moving average terms.

3. Forecasting:
   - The model is used to forecast CPU usage for the test dataset.

4. Evaluation:
  - The RMSE metric is calculated to evaluate the accuracy of the forecast.
  - A plot is generated to compare the actual test data with the forecasted values.

Output
- Root Mean Squared Error (RMSE): Indicates the accuracy of the forecast.
- Plot: A visual comparison of actual vs. predicted CPU usage values.
- CSV File: Results saved as `cpu_usage_forecast_results_arima.csv` for further analysis.

About the ARIMA Model
The ARIMA (AutoRegressive Integrated Moving Average) model is a popular statistical method for time-series forecasting. To effectively use ARIMA, understanding and tuning its parameters is crucial. The three main tuning parameters are p, d, and q.

ARIMA Parameters:
p (AutoRegressive Order): Represents the number of lag observations included in the model.
Controls the autoregression part of the model, where past values are used to predict the future.

Example: For $p=2$, the model uses the last two time points to predict the current value.
How to Tune:
- Analyze the Partial Autocorrelation Function (PACF) plot.
- Look for significant lags in the PACF to determine the value of p.

d (Differencing Order): Represents the number of times the data needs to be differenced to make it stationary. Stationarity means the statistical properties of the series (mean, variance) do not change over time.

Example: If the raw data shows a trend, differencing once ($d=1$) can remove it.
How to Tune:
- Use statistical tests like the Augmented Dickey–Fuller (ADF) test to check for stationarity. Start with $d=0$, and increase until the series is stationary.

q (Moving Average Order): Represents the number of lagged forecast errors in the model. Controls the moving average part of the model, where the model uses past errors to correct future forecasts.

Example: For $q=1$, the model uses the last error term in predictions.
How to Tune:
- Analyze the Autocorrelation Function (ACF) plot.
- Look for significant lags in the ACF to determine the value of q.

How to Tune ARIMA Parameters
Visual Inspection:
- Use ACF and PACF plots to estimate values for p, d, and q.
- Look for patterns in the data to decide on seasonal parameters.

Grid Search:
- Automate parameter tuning by testing combinations of p,d,q values. Evaluate each combination using a scoring metric like AIC (Akaike Information Criterion) or BIC (Bayesian Information Criterion).

Stationarity Check:
- Ensure the series is stationary before applying ARIMA. Use differencing (d) if necessary.

Model Diagnostics:
- Analyze residuals (errors) of the fitted model.
- Residuals should be white noise (randomly distributed with no patterns).

Cross-Validation:
- Split the time series into training and testing datasets.
- Validate model performance on unseen data to avoid overfitting.

Key Considerations
- Start with small values for p,d,q, and gradually increase based on results. Overfitting can occur if p or q values are too high.

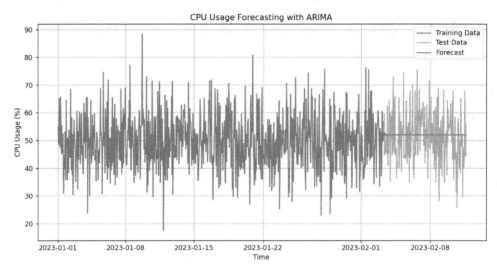

Figure 1: CPU Usage Forecasting with ARIMA

Insights and Next Steps

The ARIMA model provides a reliable method for time-series forecasting in IT operations. By identifying trends and predicting performance metrics, IT teams can proactively address potential downtimes, ensuring smooth operations and cost efficiency. This approach can be extended to other metrics, such as memory usage or disk I/O, to provide a comprehensive predictive maintenance framework.

2.5 Visualizing Predictions and Insights

Visualization is a crucial step in any data-driven project. It bridges the gap between raw data, complex models, and actionable insights, making it easier to interpret results and communicate findings effectively. In the context of predicting system downtime, visualizations can help IT teams understand patterns, evaluate model performance, and make informed decisions to enhance system reliability.

The Importance of Visualizing Predictions

1. **Enhanced Interpretability**:
   - Complex Machine Learning models like ARIMA or LSTM generate forecasts that are challenging to interpret without visual aids. Graphs and charts simplify these predictions.
   - Example: A line graph showing predicted vs. actual CPU usage over time highlights the accuracy of the forecast.
2. **Pattern Recognition**:
   - Visualizations make it easy to identify trends, seasonality, and anomalies in system performance.

- o Example: A time-series plot might reveal recurring CPU spikes during peak hours.

3. **Performance Evaluation**:
   - o Comparing actual and predicted values visually allows for quick identification of underperformance or model drift.
   - o Example: Scatter plots of residuals can indicate whether predictions are systematically biased.

4. **Actionable Insights**:
   - o IT teams can visualize when and where potential downtimes are likely, enabling proactive interventions.
   - o Example: A heatmap of predicted downtimes across systems shows critical areas needing immediate attention.

Types of Visualizations for Predictive Maintenance

1. **Line Graphs**:
   - o Use: To compare actual vs. predicted system metrics over time.
   - o Insights: Highlights deviations between forecasted and observed values.
   - o Example: A graph showing CPU usage trends and anomalies.

2. **Residual Plots**:
   - o Use: To evaluate model performance by visualizing the differences between actual and predicted values.
   - o Insights: Identifies patterns in errors, which might indicate areas for model improvement.

3. **Heatmaps**:
   - o Use: To visualize downtimes or resource bottlenecks across multiple systems or time intervals.
   - o Insights: Identifies critical systems or time periods requiring focus.

4. **Bar Charts**:
   - o Use: To summarize the frequency of downtimes or errors by category.
   - o Insights: Identifies which system components are most prone to failure.

5. **Forecast Uncertainty Plots**:
   - o Use: To display confidence intervals around predictions.
   - o Insights: Helps stakeholders assess the reliability of forecasts.

```python
import matplotlib.pyplot as plt
import pandas as pd

# Load predictions and actual data
results = pd.read_csv("cpu_usage_forecast_results_arima.csv")

# Line Graph: Actual vs. Predicted
plt.figure(figsize=(12, 6))
plt.plot(results['Actual'], label="Actual", color="blue", alpha=0.7)
plt.plot(results['Forecast'], label="Predicted", color="red",
linestyle="--")
plt.title("Actual vs. Predicted CPU Usage")
plt.xlabel("Time Steps")
plt.ylabel("CPU Usage (%)")
plt.legend()
plt.grid()
plt.show()

# Residual Plot
residuals = results['Actual'] - results['Forecast']
plt.figure(figsize=(12, 6))
plt.scatter(range(len(residuals)), residuals, color="purple",
alpha=0.6)
plt.axhline(0, color="black", linestyle="--")
plt.title("Residuals (Actual - Predicted)")
plt.xlabel("Time Steps")
plt.ylabel("Residuals")
plt.grid()
plt.show()

# Heatmap (Example Data)
import seaborn as sns
import numpy as np

# Create dummy heatmap data for downtimes
heatmap_data = np.random.randint(0, 10, size=(10, 10))
plt.figure(figsize=(10, 8))
sns.heatmap(heatmap_data, annot=True, cmap="coolwarm", cbar=True)
plt.title("Predicted Downtime Heatmap")
plt.xlabel("System ID")
plt.ylabel("Time Intervals")
plt.show()
```

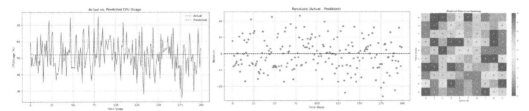

Figure 2: Sample Visual Output

Visualizing predictions is not just about creating charts—it's about translating data into actionable insights. By effectively using line graphs, residual plots, heatmaps, and other tools, IT teams can gain a deeper understanding of system performance and take proactive steps to prevent downtimes. These visualizations serve as a bridge between data-driven models and strategic decision-making, ensuring that IT operations remain reliable and efficient.

2.6 Implementing an Example using LSTM

System downtime is a critical issue in IT operations, leading to significant operational and financial losses. Predicting downtime in advance enables proactive maintenance, resource allocation, and smoother operations. The goal is to use **Long Short-Term Memory (LSTM)**, a type of recurrent neural network (RNN) specialized for time-series data, to forecast system performance metrics (e.g. CPU usage) and anticipate downtimes.

Solution Overview
1. **Input Data**:
    - o Historical system logs containing metrics such as CPU usage, memory usage, disk I/O rates, and uptime status.
2. **Preprocessing**:
    - o Normalize the data for compatibility with LSTM.
    - o Create sequences of historical values to feed into the LSTM model.
3. **Model Selection**:
    - o Use an LSTM model to capture temporal dependencies and trends in the data.
4. **Prediction**:
    - o Forecast system metrics for the next time steps.
    - o Use thresholds to classify potential downtime events based on predicted metrics.

5. **Evaluation**:
   - Assess the model's performance using metrics like Mean Squared Error (MSE) and visualization techniques.

```python
import pandas as pd
import numpy as np
import matplotlib.pyplot as plt
from sklearn.preprocessing import MinMaxScaler
from tensorflow.keras.models import Sequential
from tensorflow.keras.layers import LSTM, Dense
from sklearn.metrics import mean_squared_error

# Load the synthetic dataset
file_path = "synthetic_log_data.csv"  # Replace with your file path
log_data = pd.read_csv(file_path, parse_dates=["Timestamp"],
index_col="Timestamp")

# Select relevant metric (e.g. CPU Usage)
log_data = log_data.resample('H').mean()  # Resample to hourly
intervals if needed
cpu_usage = log_data['CPU_Usage'].fillna(method='ffill')  # Handle
missing values

# Normalize the data
scaler = MinMaxScaler(feature_range=(0, 1))
cpu_usage_scaled = scaler.fit_transform(cpu_usage.values.reshape(-
1, 1))

# Create sequences for LSTM
def create_sequences(data, sequence_length):
    X, y = [], []
    for i in range(len(data) - sequence_length):
        X.append(data[i:i + sequence_length])
        y.append(data[i + sequence_length])
    return np.array(X), np.array(y)

sequence_length = 24  # Use the past 24 hours to predict the next
value
X, y = create_sequences(cpu_usage_scaled, sequence_length)

# Split into training and testing sets
train_size = int(len(X) * 0.8)
X_train, X_test = X[:train_size], X[train_size:]
y_train, y_test = y[:train_size], y[train_size:]

# Build the LSTM model
```

```python
model = Sequential([
    LSTM(50, return_sequences=True, input_shape=(X_train.shape[1],
X_train.shape[2])),
    LSTM(50),
    Dense(1)
])

model.compile(optimizer='adam', loss='mean_squared_error')

# Train the model
history = model.fit(X_train, y_train, epochs=20, batch_size=32,
validation_data=(X_test, y_test), verbose=1)

# Make predictions
predictions = model.predict(X_test)

# Inverse transform the predictions and actual values
predictions = scaler.inverse_transform(predictions)
y_test_actual = scaler.inverse_transform(y_test.reshape(-1, 1))

# Evaluate the model
rmse = np.sqrt(mean_squared_error(y_test_actual, predictions))
print(f"Root Mean Squared Error (RMSE): {rmse}")

# Plot the results
plt.figure(figsize=(12, 6))
plt.plot(y_test_actual, label="Actual", color="blue")
plt.plot(predictions, label="Predicted", color="red", linestyle="--
")
plt.title("CPU Usage Prediction with LSTM")
plt.xlabel("Time Steps")
plt.ylabel("CPU Usage (%)")
plt.legend()
plt.grid()
plt.show()

# Save predictions to a CSV file
forecast_df = pd.DataFrame({"Actual": y_test_actual.flatten(),
"Predicted": predictions.flatten()})
forecast_df.to_csv("lstm_predictions.csv", index=False)

print("Prediction results saved to 'lstm_predictions.csv'.")
```

Explanation of the Steps
1. **Data Preparation**:
   - The data is normalized to ensure compatibility with the LSTM model, which performs better with values in a uniform range (e.g. 0 to 1).
   - Sequences of historical values are created to capture temporal dependencies.
2. **Model Design**:
   - The LSTM model has two LSTM layers to capture long-term and short-term dependencies in the time-series data.
   - A dense output layer predicts the next value in the series.
3. **Training and Testing**:
   - The dataset is split into training (80%) and testing (20%) sets to evaluate model performance on unseen data.
   - The model is trained using Adam optimizer and mean_squared_error loss.
4. **Evaluation**:
   - The RMSE metric quantifies the difference between actual and predicted values.
   - Visualization of actual vs. predicted values helps assess the model's performance.

Output and Insights
- **Root Mean Squared Error (RMSE)**:
  - A lower RMSE indicates better model performance.
- **Visualization**:
  - The line graph compares actual vs. predicted CPU usage, showing how well the model captures trends.
- **Proactive Maintenance**:
  - If the predicted CPU usage exceeds a predefined threshold, it signals potential downtime, enabling proactive actions.

By leveraging LSTM for time-series forecasting, IT teams can effectively predict system performance metrics and anticipate downtimes. This approach provides actionable insights, allowing organizations to optimize resource allocation, reduce operational disruptions, and improve overall system reliability. As a next step, you can extend this solution to incorporate additional metrics like memory usage and disk I/O rates for a more comprehensive predictive maintenance framework.

2.7 Challenges and Best Practices

As organizations increasingly adopt Machine Learning models like ARIMA and LSTM for IT operations, they face a mix of challenges and opportunities. Addressing these challenges through best practices can ensure the success and reliability of predictive maintenance systems.

Challenges in Implementing Predictive Models

1. **Data Quality and Availability**:
   - **Challenge**: Predictive models rely on high-quality historical data. Inconsistent, incomplete, or noisy data can significantly degrade model performance.
   - **Example**: Missing log entries or inaccurate timestamps can lead to incorrect forecasts.
   - **Impact**: Poor data quality results in unreliable predictions, undermining the trust in predictive systems.

2. **Model Selection and Complexity**:
   - **Challenge**: Choosing the right model (e.g. ARIMA, LSTM) requires expertise and an understanding of the problem domain.
   - **Example**: A simple ARIMA model might work for linear trends but struggle with non-linear or seasonal data, necessitating more complex models like LSTM.
   - **Impact**: Misaligned models can lead to underfitting, overfitting, or irrelevant predictions.

3. **Interpretability of Results**:
   - **Challenge**: Complex models, especially deep learning ones like LSTM, often function as "black boxes," making it hard to interpret results.
   - **Example**: While LSTM may predict downtime accurately, understanding *why* a system might fail remains elusive.
   - **Impact**: Lack of transparency can reduce stakeholder confidence in the system.

4. **Scalability and Real-Time Requirements**:
   - **Challenge**: IT systems generate vast amounts of data, and models must process this information in real-time.

- o **Example**: A model trained on batch data may not perform well in a streaming environment.
- o **Impact**: Delayed insights can render predictions ineffective for proactive maintenance.

5. **Resource Constraints**:
- o **Challenge**: Deploying and maintaining Machine Learning models require computational resources and skilled personnel.
- o **Example**: Training LSTM models can be computationally intensive, necessitating robust infrastructure.
- o **Impact**: Organizations with limited resources may struggle to implement and sustain predictive systems.

Best Practices for Successful Implementation
1. **Ensure High-Quality Data**:
- o **Practice**: Regularly clean, preprocess, and validate data before feeding it into predictive models.
- o **Tools**: Use data cleaning libraries like pandas and visualization tools like matplotlib to identify anomalies.
- o **Outcome**: Reliable data leads to accurate and actionable predictions.

2. **Align Models with Business Goals**:
- o **Practice**: Choose models based on the specific requirements of the IT operation.
- o **Example**: Use ARIMA for linear trends and LSTM for capturing long-term dependencies and seasonality.
- o **Outcome**: Tailored models ensure better alignment with organizational needs.

3. **Invest in Explainability**:
- o **Practice**: Use techniques like SHAP (SHapley Additive exPlanations) or LIME (Local Interpretable Model-agnostic Explanations) to make model outputs interpretable.
- o **Outcome**: Transparent predictions build trust and facilitate informed decision-making.

4. **Leverage Scalable Infrastructure**:

- o **Practice**: Use cloud-based platforms like AWS, Azure, or Google Cloud for scalability and real-time processing.

- o **Outcome**: Efficient handling of large datasets and real-time analytics ensures timely insights.

5. **Monitor and Maintain Models**:

- o **Practice**: Continuously monitor model performance and retrain with updated data to prevent model drift.

- o **Outcome**: Sustained accuracy and relevance of predictive systems over time.

6. **Train Teams and Stakeholders**:

- o **Practice**: Provide training for IT teams and stakeholders to understand the models and their implications.

- o **Outcome**: A well-informed team ensures smooth implementation and adoption.

Conclusion and Takeaways

Predictive modelling in IT operations is a transformative approach that empowers organizations to anticipate system downtimes, optimize resources, and enhance overall reliability. However, implementing these systems comes with its challenges, including data quality issues, scalability concerns, and resource constraints. By adopting best practices such as ensuring data integrity, choosing the right models, investing in explainability, and leveraging scalable infrastructure, these hurdles can be effectively addressed.

Key takeaways from this chapter include:

- **Proactive Maintenance**: Predictive models enable organizations to transition from reactive to proactive maintenance, minimizing disruptions and costs.

- **Continuous Improvement**: Model performance should be continuously monitored and updated to align with evolving IT landscapes.

- **Strategic Advantage**: Organizations that embrace predictive modelling gain a competitive edge by improving operational efficiency and reliability.

Ultimately, the road to effective predictive maintenance lies in balancing technological advancements with practical implementation strategies. As we move forward, understanding the challenges and adhering to best practices will be crucial in unlocking the full potential of predictive models for IT operations.

* * *

Anomaly Detection
For Real-Time Monitoring

CHAPTER 3

ANOMALY DETECTION FOR REAL-TIME MONITORING

In the fast-paced world of IT operations, ensuring system stability and uptime is crucial. Real-time anomaly detection plays a pivotal role in achieving this goal by identifying irregularities in system behavior that could indicate potential issues. Unlike traditional monitoring methods that rely on predefined thresholds or manual inspections, anomaly detection leverages advanced algorithms to autonomously recognize unexpected patterns, enabling IT teams to act proactively rather than reactively.

By end of this chapter, readers will:
- Understand the concept and importance of anomaly detection in IT operations.
- Gain hands-on experience with Isolation Forest and Autoencoders for anomaly detection.
- Be able to identify and visualize anomalies in real-time data to prevent system failures.
- Learn best practices for implementing, evaluating, and maintaining anomaly detection systems.

Let's dive in!

3.1 Introduction to Real-Time Anomaly Detection

Anomaly detection is the process of identifying data points or patterns that deviate significantly from the norm. In IT operations, these anomalies often manifest as sudden spikes in CPU usage, unexpected drops in network throughput, or irregular disk I/O patterns. Real-time anomaly detection extends this concept by monitoring live data streams, allowing for immediate identification of potential issues as they arise.

For example:
- A sudden increase in memory usage could indicate a memory leak in an application.
- An abrupt drop in network bandwidth might signal a hardware failure or a cyberattack.

- Irregular patterns in disk read/write speeds may point to storage degradation.

Real-time anomaly detection systems analyze these patterns and trigger alerts or automated actions, enabling IT teams to address issues before they escalate into critical failures.

Why is Real-Time Anomaly Detection Important?

1. **Proactive Issue Resolution**:
   - Traditional monitoring tools often detect problems only after they have caused significant disruption. Real-time anomaly detection allows teams to identify and address anomalies before they impact system performance.
   - Example: Detecting a CPU spike caused by an infinite loop in a program before it crashes the system.

2. **Minimizing Downtime**:
   - Downtime in IT systems leads to financial losses, reduced customer satisfaction, and tarnished brand reputation. By identifying anomalies early, organizations can reduce the likelihood of prolonged outages.
   - Example: Identifying unusual network latency that could lead to a server outage during peak traffic.

3. **Enhancing Security**:
   - Many cyberattacks, such as distributed denial-of-service (DDoS) attacks or unauthorized data breaches, manifest as anomalies in system metrics. Real-time detection helps in identifying and mitigating such threats promptly.
   - Example: Detecting unusual spikes in network traffic that could indicate a DDoS attack.

4. **Optimizing Resource Utilization**:
   - Anomalies in resource usage can signal inefficiencies or over-provisioning. Real-time monitoring enables better resource allocation and cost optimization.
   - Example: Spotting underutilized server resources during non-peak hours for load redistribution.

Traditional Methods vs. Real-Time Anomaly Detection

1. **Threshold-Based Monitoring**:
   - Relies on static thresholds set manually for metrics like CPU usage or memory consumption.

      o Limitation: Cannot adapt to changing patterns or unforeseen scenarios, leading to false positives or missed anomalies.
2. **Rule-Based Systems**:
      o Use pre-defined rules to detect specific conditions.
      o Limitation: Requires extensive domain knowledge and fails to handle dynamic and complex data.
3. **Machine Learning-Based Anomaly Detection**:
      o Adapts to evolving patterns in real-time data streams.
      o Can detect subtle and complex anomalies that traditional methods might overlook.

Applications of Real-Time Anomaly Detection in IT Operations
1. **Predictive Maintenance**:
      o Identify early warning signs of hardware or software failures.
      o Example: Detecting abnormal disk read/write speeds to predict storage device failure.
2. **Performance Optimization**:
      o Monitor system performance in real-time and detect bottlenecks.
      o Example: Identifying increased database query response times during peak usage.
3. **Incident Management**:
      o Reduce the mean time to detect (MTTD) and mean time to resolve (MTTR) incidents.
      o Example: Detecting sudden spikes in error rates in a web application.
4. **Fraud Detection**:
      o Identify suspicious activities or unauthorized access in real-time.
      o Example: Spotting anomalous login attempts outside business hours.

A Simple Example
Imagine a large e-commerce platform that monitors its IT infrastructure in real-time. During a promotional sale, traffic surges dramatically, causing CPU usage and network latency to increase. Traditional monitoring tools might struggle to differentiate between normal peak-time behavior and an actual anomaly. However, a real-time anomaly detection system, trained on historical traffic patterns, identifies:
- A specific server node experiencing an unusually high error rate.
- A database query running much slower than expected.

This early detection allows the IT team to address these issues promptly, ensuring a seamless customer experience during a critical business event.

Real-time anomaly detection is a cornerstone of modern IT operations, enabling organizations to maintain system stability, enhance security, and optimize performance. By leveraging advanced algorithms and Machine Learning techniques, IT teams can move beyond reactive troubleshooting to proactive maintenance. In the subsequent sections, we will delve into the types of metrics used for anomaly detection, the algorithms that power these systems, and how to implement a robust anomaly detection pipeline tailored for real-time IT environments.

3.2 Understanding Real-Time Monitoring Metrics

In IT operations, metrics are the pulse of your infrastructure, providing a continuous flow of information about system performance, health, and reliability. Real-time monitoring metrics are fundamental for detecting anomalies, predicting failures, and ensuring optimal operations. Understanding these metrics is essential to set the foundation for effective anomaly detection and proactive maintenance.

What Are Real-Time Monitoring Metrics?

Real-time monitoring metrics are continuous measurements that reflect the state and performance of IT systems. They encompass a wide range of data points collected from servers, applications, networks, and other components of an IT infrastructure. These metrics serve as indicators for normal operations and potential issues.

Categories of Real-Time Monitoring Metrics
1. System Performance Metrics:

1. CPU Usage: Measures the percentage of CPU resources being utilized.
   Example: A server experiencing high CPU usage (>90%) for an extended period may indicate an overloaded application or a runaway process.
2. Memory Usage: Tracks the percentage of system memory in use.
   Example: A memory spike might signal a memory leak in an application or excessive caching.
3. Disk I/O Rate: Reflects the read/write speed of the storage subsystem.
   Example: High disk I/O could indicate inefficient queries or database performance issues.

2. Network Metrics:

1. Network Latency: The time it takes for a data packet to travel between two points.
    Example: Increased latency might indicate network congestion or hardware issues.
2. Packet Loss: The percentage of data packets lost during transmission.
    Example: High packet loss could be due to a failing network device or a cyberattack.
3. Bandwidth Utilization: The percentage of available network capacity being used.
    Example: Spikes in bandwidth usage might indicate a DDoS attack or heavy data transfers.

3. Application-Specific Metrics:

1. Request/Response Times: Tracks how long an application takes to handle requests.
    Example: Prolonged response times in a web application may suggest a backend bottleneck.
2. Error Rates: Measures the frequency of application errors.
    Example: A sudden increase in 500-series HTTP errors could point to server-side issues.
3. Throughput: The number of successful transactions or processes per second.
    Example: A drop in throughput could indicate system overload or degraded performance.

4. Service Metrics:

1. Uptime Status: Indicates whether a service is operational or down.
    Example: Frequent downtimes in a service might suggest hardware failure or insufficient capacity.
2. Queue Depth: Tracks the number of pending tasks or requests in a queue.
    Example: High queue depth may signify resource contention or inefficient task management.

5. Custom Metrics:

1. Metrics tailored to specific use cases or applications.
    Example: A retail application might monitor "Items Purchased Per Minute" during peak sales events.

Characteristics of Real-Time Monitoring Metrics

High Velocity:

- Real-time metrics are generated continuously, often at millisecond intervals.
- Systems must process and store this high-speed data efficiently.

Variability:

- Metrics fluctuate based on workloads, user activity, and external factors like network traffic.
- Distinguishing normal variability from true anomalies is critical.

Interdependence:

- Metrics often influence each other. For example, high CPU usage might correlate with increased memory usage.
- Analyzing these interdependencies can improve anomaly detection accuracy.

Noisiness:

- Metrics may contain noise due to temporary spikes or system idiosyncrasies.
- Proper preprocessing is needed to filter out irrelevant fluctuations.

The Role of Metrics in Anomaly Detection

Real-time monitoring metrics are the foundation of anomaly detection. By continuously analyzing these metrics, systems can:

Establish Baselines:
- Determine what constitutes normal behavior under typical operating conditions.
- *Example*: CPU usage averaging 50% with occasional spikes during peak hours.

Identify Deviations:
- Detect patterns that deviate significantly from the baseline.
- *Example*: A sudden spike to 100% CPU usage outside expected peak hours.

Trigger Alerts:
- Automatically notify IT teams of potential issues for immediate investigation.

- *Example*: An alert triggered when memory usage exceeds 90% for 10 consecutive minutes.

Challenges in Monitoring Real-Time Metrics

Data Overload:
- Real-time monitoring generates vast amounts of data, making it challenging to process and analyze in real-time.
- *Solution*: Use streaming analytics frameworks like Apache Kafka or Spark Streaming.

False Positives/Negatives:
- Static thresholds often result in false alarms or missed anomalies.
- *Solution*: Employ Machine Learning techniques to dynamically learn and adapt baselines.

Integration Across Systems:
- Collecting and consolidating metrics from diverse systems and tools can be complex.
- *Solution*: Use centralized monitoring platforms like Prometheus, Grafana, or Datadog.

Latency in Alerts:
- Delays in analyzing metrics can lead to late detection of critical issues.
- *Solution*: Optimize pipeline latency using real-time processing and low-latency architectures.

3.3 Data Preparation for Anomaly Detection

Data preparation is a critical step in building an anomaly detection system. High-quality, well-prepared data ensures that Machine Learning models can accurately detect and classify anomalies in real-time monitoring metrics. This section explores the key steps involved in preparing data for anomaly detection, including data cleaning, feature engineering, normalization, and the creation of a synthetic dataset suitable for the analyses discussed in this chapter.

Steps in Data Preparation
1. **Data Cleaning:**
   - Remove or handle missing values, outliers, and inconsistencies.
   - Ensure timestamp alignment for time-series data.

2. **Feature Engineering**:
    o   Extract meaningful features from raw data, such as averages, rates, or time lags.
    o   Create derived metrics like CPU-to-memory usage ratios or network throughput per active connection.
3. **Normalization and Scaling**:
    o   Normalize data to a uniform scale to improve model performance.
    o   Example: Scale all metrics between 0 and 1 for neural networks or between -1 and 1 for algorithms like Isolation Forest.
4. **Segmentation**:
    o   Segment data into windows for time-series analysis.
    o   Example: Use sliding windows of 24 hours to detect anomalies based on past trends.

Understanding the Dataset

1. **Columns**:
    o   *Timestamp*: Date and time for each observation.
    o   *CPU_Usage*: Percentage of CPU resources being used.
    o   *Memory_Usage*: Percentage of system memory in use.
    o   *Disk_IO_Rate*: Rate of disk input/output operations.
    o   *Network_Latency*: Time taken for a packet to travel between nodes.
    o   *Anomaly*: Binary label indicating normal (0) or anomalous (1) behavior.
2. **Injected Anomalies**:
    o   5% of the data contains anomalies, simulating real-world conditions where anomalies are rare but critical.
3. **Usage**:
    o   Suitable for training and testing Machine Learning models like Isolation Forest, Autoencoders, or LSTM.
    o   Can be used to evaluate the performance of algorithms in identifying anomalies.

Working with the Dataset:
Work with the dataset to understand the nature of the data.

```
# Import libraries
import pandas as pd
import numpy as np
```

```
# Loading and Cleaning Data:
data = pd.read_csv("anomaly_detection_data.csv")
data = data.fillna(method="ffill")  # Forward fill missing values
'''
Feature Engineering:
Create new features like rolling averages or differences to capture
trends and sudden changes.
'''
data['CPU_Rolling_Mean'] =
data['CPU_Usage'].rolling(window=5).mean()
data['Memory_Diff'] = data['Memory_Usage'].diff()


'''
Normalization:

Normalize metrics for compatibility with algorithms.
'''
from sklearn.preprocessing import MinMaxScaler
scaler = MinMaxScaler()
data[['CPU_Usage', 'Memory_Usage', 'Disk_IO_Rate',
'Network_Latency']] = scaler.fit_transform(
    data[['CPU_Usage', 'Memory_Usage', 'Disk_IO_Rate',
'Network_Latency']]
)


'''
Segmentation for Time-Series Models:

Create sliding windows for temporal analysis.
'''
def create_sequences(data, sequence_length):
    X, y = [], []
    for i in range(len(data) - sequence_length):
        X.append(data[i:i + sequence_length, :-1])
        y.append(data[i + sequence_length, -1])
    return np.array(X), np.array(y)

sequence_length = 24  # Use 24-hour sequences
X, y = create_sequences(data.values, sequence_length)


'''
Visualizing the Dataset
Plotting Metrics Over Time:
'''

import matplotlib.pyplot as plt

plt.figure(figsize=(12, 6))
```

```
plt.plot(data['Timestamp'], data['CPU_Usage'], label='CPU Usage')
plt.plot(data['Timestamp'], data['Memory_Usage'], label='Memory
Usage')
plt.title("System Metrics Over Time")
plt.xlabel("Time")
plt.ylabel("Usage (%)")
plt.legend()
plt.grid()
plt.show()

#Highlighting Anomalies:

plt.figure(figsize=(12, 6))
plt.scatter(data['Timestamp'], data['CPU_Usage'],
c=data['Anomaly'], cmap='coolwarm', label='Anomalies')
plt.title("CPU Usage with Anomalies Highlighted")
plt.xlabel("Time")
plt.ylabel("CPU Usage (%)")
plt.legend()
plt.grid()
plt.show()
```

3.4 Introduction to Anomaly Detection Algorithms

Anomaly detection algorithms are the backbone of any system designed to identify irregularities in data. These algorithms enable IT operations teams to detect unusual patterns in system metrics, helping to prevent potential system failures, optimize resource usage, and enhance overall efficiency. In this section, we delve into the fundamentals of anomaly detection algorithms, explore different types, and discuss their relevance to IT operations management.

What Is Anomaly Detection?

Anomaly detection is the process of identifying data points, events, or patterns that deviate significantly from the expected norm. In the context of IT operations, anomalies could represent:

- A sudden spike in CPU usage.
- A drastic drop in network throughput.
- Unusually high disk I/O activity.

These deviations often indicate potential issues such as hardware failures, software bugs, security breaches, or inefficiencies. Effective anomaly detection systems enable organizations to address these problems proactively.

Why Are Anomaly Detection Algorithms Important?

1. **Proactive Issue Resolution:**

- o Anomalies often precede critical failures. Detecting them early minimizes downtime and reduces costs.
- o Example: Identifying a memory leak through unusual memory consumption trends.

2. **Enhanced Security**:
   - o Many cyberattacks manifest as anomalies in system metrics.
   - o Example: Detecting unauthorized login attempts outside business hours.

3. **Resource Optimization**:
   - o Detecting inefficiencies or overutilization of resources allows for better allocation.
   - o Example: Spotting servers running at near-zero utilization.

4. **Scalability**:
   - o Modern IT systems generate massive volumes of data. Automated anomaly detection scales effortlessly to handle this data, unlike manual monitoring.

Types of Anomaly Detection Algorithms

1. **Statistical Methods**:
   - o Rely on mathematical models to identify data points that deviate from expected distributions.
   - o **Examples**:
     - • Z-Score: Flags data points that are several standard deviations away from the mean.
     - • Moving Averages: Identifies deviations in rolling averages.
   - o **Advantages**:
     - • Simple and fast for structured data.
   - o **Limitations**:
     - • May fail to capture complex patterns or seasonal trends.

2. **Machine Learning-Based Methods**:
   - o Use algorithms to learn patterns from data and identify deviations.
   - o **Examples**:
     - • **Supervised Learning**:
       - • Requires labeled data (normal vs. anomalous).
       - • Algorithms: Random Forest, Support Vector Machines (SVM).
     - • **Unsupervised Learning**:
       - • Does not require labeled data, making it suitable for IT logs with rare anomalies.

- Algorithms: Isolation Forest, k-Means Clustering.
  - o **Advantages**:
    - Captures complex patterns.
  - o **Limitations**:
    - Requires significant computational resources.
3. **Deep Learning-Based Methods**:
   - o Leverages neural networks to model non-linear relationships and identify subtle anomalies.
   - o **Examples**:
     - Autoencoders: Reconstruct input data and identify anomalies through reconstruction errors.
     - Long Short-Term Memory (LSTM): Ideal for time-series data, capturing sequential dependencies.
   - o **Advantages**:
     - Handles large datasets and complex relationships.
   - o **Limitations**:
     - High computational cost and longer training times.
4. **Proximity-Based Methods**:
   - o Identify anomalies by measuring distances between data points in feature space.
   - o **Examples**:
     - k-Nearest Neighbors (k-NN): Flags points far from their nearest neighbors.
     - Density-Based Spatial Clustering of Applications with Noise (DBSCAN): Identifies sparse points in dense clusters.
   - o **Advantages**:
     - Effective for small datasets.
   - o **Limitations**:
     - Struggles with high-dimensional data.

Popular Anomaly Detection Algorithms for IT Operations
1. **Isolation Forest**:
   - o Splits data points recursively to isolate anomalies faster than normal points.
   - o **Use Case**: Detecting unusual spikes in CPU or memory usage.
2. **Autoencoders**:
   - o Train a neural network to reconstruct normal data, using reconstruction errors to identify anomalies.

- o **Use Case**: Identifying subtle deviations in system logs or application performance metrics.
3. **LSTM Networks**:
   - o Leverage time-series data to capture temporal dependencies and identify anomalies.
   - o **Use Case**: Detecting unusual trends in network latency over time.
4. **Statistical Methods**:
   - o Moving averages combined with standard deviation thresholds.
   - o **Use Case**: Simple anomaly detection in disk I/O rates.

Selecting the Right Algorithm
1. **Nature of Data**:
   - o **Structured Data**: Statistical methods and Machine Learning are effective.
   - o **Unstructured Data**: Deep learning methods, such as autoencoders, perform better.
2. **Volume of Data**:
   - o **Small Datasets**: Statistical methods or proximity-based methods like k-NN.
   - o **Large Datasets**: Machine Learning and deep learning methods.
3. **Complexity of Patterns**:
   - o **Simple Patterns**: Statistical methods or Isolation Forest.
   - o **Complex Patterns**: Autoencoders or LSTM.

A Practical Perspective
In IT operations, the choice of algorithm often depends on:
- **Accuracy Needs**: High accuracy may warrant deep learning models, while moderate accuracy might suffice with simpler methods.
- **Resource Availability**: Computationally lightweight algorithms are better suited for environments with limited infrastructure.
- **Real-Time Constraints**: Algorithms like Isolation Forest can work efficiently in real-time scenarios.

Anomaly detection algorithms are indispensable for maintaining system health and reliability in IT operations. In the next sections, we'll delve deeper into implementing Isolation Forest and Autoencoders for anomaly detection, equipping you with practical skills to apply these algorithms effectively.

3.5 Implementing Anomaly Detection using Isolation Forest

Objective
To identify anomalies in real-time system metrics such as CPU usage, memory usage, disk I/O rates, and network latency using the Isolation Forest algorithm. These anomalies could indicate potential issues such as hardware failures, software bugs, or security threats.

Scenario
A company's IT operations team wants to monitor system performance in real time to prevent downtime. The team observes that certain metrics (e.g. CPU usage or network latency) occasionally spike, leading to system degradation. The objective is to use Isolation Forest to detect these anomalous patterns, enabling the team to address potential issues proactively.

Solution Approach
1. **Dataset Preparation**:
    o   Use the synthetic dataset generated earlier, which includes system metrics (CPU_Usage, Memory_Usage, Disk_IO_Rate, and Network_Latency) along with a timestamp.
    o   Label anomalies based on known injected irregularities in the dataset.
2. **Algorithm Overview**:
    o   Isolation Forest works by isolating data points through recursive partitioning.
    o   Anomalies are isolated quickly, as they lie far from dense regions of normal data.
3. **Implementation Steps**:
    o   Load the dataset and preprocess it.
    o   Normalize the data to improve algorithm performance.
    o   Train the Isolation Forest model on the data.
    o   Predict anomalies and visualize the results.
4. **Outcome**:
    o   Identify anomalous data points in the metrics.
    o   Highlight these anomalies on visualizations for further analysis.

Implementation

```python
import pandas as pd
import numpy as np
from sklearn.ensemble import IsolationForest
from sklearn.preprocessing import MinMaxScaler
import matplotlib.pyplot as plt

# Step 1: Load the Dataset
data = pd.read_csv("anomaly_detection_data.csv",
parse_dates=["Timestamp"])
data.set_index("Timestamp", inplace=True)

# Step 2: Preprocess the Data
# Normalize the metrics
scaler = MinMaxScaler()
normalized_data = scaler.fit_transform(data[['CPU_Usage',
'Memory_Usage', 'Disk_IO_Rate', 'Network_Latency']])

# Step 3: Train the Isolation Forest Model
model = IsolationForest(n_estimators=100, contamination=0.05,
random_state=42)
data['Anomaly_Predicted'] = model.fit_predict(normalized_data)

# Anomalies are labeled as -1, normal data as 1
data['Anomaly_Predicted'] = data['Anomaly_Predicted'].apply(lambda
x: 1 if x == -1 else 0)

# Step 4: Visualize the Results
# Plot CPU Usage with anomalies highlighted
plt.figure(figsize=(12, 6))
plt.plot(data.index, data['CPU_Usage'], label='CPU Usage',
color='blue', alpha=0.7)
plt.scatter(
    data.index[data['Anomaly_Predicted'] == 1],
    data['CPU_Usage'][data['Anomaly_Predicted'] == 1],
    color='red',
    label='Anomalies'
)
plt.title("CPU Usage with Anomalies Detected by Isolation Forest")
plt.xlabel("Timestamp")
plt.ylabel("CPU Usage (%)")
plt.legend()
plt.grid()
plt.show()

# Plot all metrics to show anomalies
```

```
fig, axs = plt.subplots(4, 1, figsize=(12, 16), sharex=True)
metrics = ['CPU_Usage', 'Memory_Usage', 'Disk_IO_Rate',
'Network_Latency']
for i, metric in enumerate(metrics):
    axs[i].plot(data.index, data[metric], label=metric,
color='blue', alpha=0.7)
    axs[i].scatter(
        data.index[data['Anomaly_Predicted'] == 1],
        data[metric][data['Anomaly_Predicted'] == 1],
        color='red',
        label='Anomalies'
    )
    axs[i].set_title(f"{metric} with Anomalies")
    axs[i].set_ylabel(metric)
    axs[i].legend()
    axs[i].grid()
plt.xlabel("Timestamp")
plt.show()


# Save predictions to a CSV file
data.to_csv("isolation_forest_predictions.csv", index=False)
```

Explanation of the Code
1. **Data Loading and Preprocessing**:
    o The dataset is loaded, and only relevant metrics are selected.
    o Data is normalized using MinMaxScaler to bring all metrics to a uniform scale.
2. **Training the Isolation Forest Model**:
    o IsolationForest is initialized with contamination=0.05, which means we expect approximately 5% of the data points to be anomalies.
    o The model learns the patterns of normal behavior in the metrics and assigns anomaly scores.
3. **Anomaly Prediction**:
    o Anomalies are labeled as 1 and normal points as 0 in the Anomaly_Predicted column.
4. **Visualization**:
    o Anomalies are highlighted on plots for each metric. Red points indicate detected anomalies.

Output
  1. **CPU Usage Plot**:
      o Shows the CPU usage over time with anomalies highlighted in red.
      o Anomalies correspond to spikes or unusual dips in CPU usage.
  2. **Combined Metrics Visualization**:
      o Each metric is plotted separately, showing detected anomalies across Memory_Usage, Disk_IO_Rate, and Network_Latency.

Outcome
  - The Isolation Forest model successfully identifies anomalous data points in the system metrics.
  - These anomalies can be investigated further to determine root causes, such as hardware issues, software bugs, or potential security threats.

Isolation Forest provides an efficient and scalable solution for detecting anomalies in IT operations data. By automating the identification of unusual patterns, this approach enables IT teams to focus on resolving critical issues proactively, reducing downtime, and improving system reliability. This implementation demonstrates how Machine Learning can transform IT operations by enabling real-time anomaly detection.

3.6 Implementing Anomaly Detection using Autoencoders
Objective
To identify anomalies in real-time system metrics such as CPU usage, memory usage, disk I/O rates, and network latency using an Autoencoder. Autoencoders are particularly effective for detecting subtle anomalies by learning the normal patterns in the data and identifying deviations as reconstruction errors.

Scenario
An IT operations team needs a robust anomaly detection system for their infrastructure. Metrics such as CPU usage, memory utilization, disk I/O rates, and network latency need to be continuously monitored. The team aims to use Autoencoders to model normal system behavior and flag anomalies when the reconstruction error exceeds a predefined threshold.

Solution Approach

1. **Dataset Preparation**:
   - Use the synthetic dataset created earlier, containing metrics (CPU_Usage, Memory_Usage, Disk_IO_Rate, Network_Latency) with injected anomalies.
2. **Algorithm Overview**:
   - Autoencoders are neural networks trained to reconstruct input data. They encode the data into a compressed representation and decode it back to the original format.
   - Anomalies result in high reconstruction errors as the model struggles to recreate patterns it hasn't seen during training.
3. **Implementation Steps**:
   - Normalize the dataset.
   - Split the data into training (normal data) and test sets (including anomalies).
   - Train an Autoencoder on the normal data to learn typical system behavior.
   - Use the model to reconstruct test data and calculate reconstruction errors.
   - Flag anomalies based on a reconstruction error threshold.
4. **Outcome**:
   - Identify abnormal patterns in system metrics that could indicate potential failures.

Implementation

```python
import pandas as pd
import numpy as np
import matplotlib.pyplot as plt
from sklearn.preprocessing import MinMaxScaler
from tensorflow.keras.models import Sequential
from tensorflow.keras.layers import Dense

# Step 1: Load the Dataset
data = pd.read_csv("anomaly_detection_data.csv",
parse_dates=["Timestamp"])
data.set_index("Timestamp", inplace=True)

# Step 2: Normalize the Data
scaler = MinMaxScaler()
normalized_data = scaler.fit_transform(data[['CPU_Usage',
```

```python
'Memory_Usage', 'Disk_IO_Rate', 'Network_Latency']])

# Step 3: Split Data into Training and Testing Sets
train_data = normalized_data[data['Anomaly'] == 0]  # Only normal
data for training
test_data = normalized_data  # Include anomalies for testing

# Step 4: Build the Autoencoder Model
input_dim = train_data.shape[1]

autoencoder = Sequential([
    Dense(16, activation='relu', input_shape=(input_dim,)),
    Dense(8, activation='relu'),
    Dense(16, activation='relu'),
    Dense(input_dim, activation='sigmoid')
])

autoencoder.compile(optimizer='adam', loss='mse')

# Step 5: Train the Autoencoder
autoencoder.fit(train_data, train_data, epochs=50, batch_size=32,
validation_split=0.1, verbose=1)

# Step 6: Reconstruct Test Data
reconstructed_data = autoencoder.predict(test_data)
reconstruction_errors = np.mean(np.square(test_data -
reconstructed_data), axis=1)

# Step 7: Set Threshold for Anomalies
threshold = np.percentile(reconstruction_errors, 95)  # Top 5% of
errors
data['Anomaly_Predicted'] = (reconstruction_errors >
threshold).astype(int)

# Save reconstruction errors to a CSV file
reconstruction_error_df = pd.DataFrame({
    "Timestamp": data.index,
    "Reconstruction_Error": reconstruction_errors,
    "Threshold": [threshold] * len(reconstruction_errors),
    "Anomaly_Predicted": data['Anomaly_Predicted']
})
reconstruction_error_df.to_csv("autoencoder_reconstruction_errors.c
sv", index=False)

# Step 8: Visualize Results
# Plot CPU Usage with anomalies highlighted
plt.figure(figsize=(12, 6))
plt.plot(data.index, data['CPU_Usage'], label='CPU Usage',
```

```
color='blue', alpha=0.7)
plt.scatter(
    data.index[data['Anomaly_Predicted'] == 1],
    data['CPU_Usage'][data['Anomaly_Predicted'] == 1],
    color='red',
    label='Anomalies'
)
plt.title("CPU Usage with Anomalies Detected by Autoencoder")
plt.xlabel("Timestamp")
plt.ylabel("CPU Usage (%)")
plt.legend()
plt.grid()
plt.show()

# Plot reconstruction errors
plt.figure(figsize=(12, 6))
plt.plot(data.index, reconstruction_errors, label='Reconstruction
Error', color='green')
plt.axhline(y=threshold, color='red', linestyle='--',
label='Threshold')
plt.title("Reconstruction Errors for Test Data")
plt.xlabel("Timestamp")
plt.ylabel("Reconstruction Error")
plt.legend()
plt.grid()
plt.show()

# Save predictions to a CSV file
data.to_csv("autoencoder_predictions.csv", index=False)
```

Explanation of the Code

1. **Data Preparation**:
   - Normalize metrics for improved training and testing performance.
   - Train the Autoencoder only on normal data to ensure it learns the usual system patterns.
2. **Autoencoder Design**:
   - A three-layer neural network compresses the data and then reconstructs it.
   - The output layer uses a sigmoid activation function to match the normalized data range.

3. **Reconstruction Error**:
    o Anomalies are identified based on reconstruction errors. If the error exceeds the threshold, the data point is flagged as an anomaly.

4. **Threshold Selection**:
    o A percentile-based threshold (e.g. 95th percentile) ensures only significant anomalies are flagged.

Output
1. **CPU Usage Plot**:
    o Shows CPU usage over time, with anomalies highlighted in red.
    o Clear identification of spikes or irregularities as anomalies.
2. **Reconstruction Error Plot**:
    o Displays reconstruction errors for the test data.
    o Points above the threshold are flagged as anomalies.

Outcome
- The Autoencoder successfully identifies anomalies in the system metrics by detecting reconstruction errors beyond the threshold.
- This method is particularly effective for detecting subtle or complex anomalies that traditional methods may miss.

Autoencoders provide a powerful, flexible approach for anomaly detection in IT operations, especially for high-dimensional or complex data. By learning normal patterns and flagging deviations, they enable proactive anomaly detection, reducing downtime and improving system reliability. This implementation demonstrates how neural networks can be leveraged to tackle challenging anomaly detection tasks in real-world scenarios.

3.7 Visualizing Anomalies

Visualization plays a crucial role in anomaly detection as it transforms raw data and model outputs into actionable insights. It enables IT operations teams to quickly identify patterns, understand model performance, and compare the results of different algorithms. This section focuses on visualizing the outputs and errors of Isolation Forest and Autoencoder models, along with a comparison of their performance in detecting anomalies.

Why Visualization Is Important
1. **Interpretability**: Helps non-technical stakeholders understand system performance and anomalies.
2. **Pattern Recognition**: Highlights trends and outliers in system metrics, making anomalies easier to spot.
3. **Algorithm Comparison**: Assists in evaluating and comparing the results of different anomaly detection models.

Visualization Objectives
1. Highlight detected anomalies on system metrics for both Isolation Forest and Autoencoder models.
2. Visualize reconstruction errors from the Autoencoder.
3. Compare the anomaly detection results from both models to evaluate their effectiveness.

Implementing Visualization

```python
import matplotlib.pyplot as plt
import pandas as pd

# Load the main dataset
data = pd.read_csv("anomaly_detection_data.csv",
parse_dates=["Timestamp"])
data.set_index("Timestamp", inplace=True)
'''
Reads the main dataset containing system metrics (e.g. CPU_Usage,
Memory_Usage) and sets the Timestamp column as the index for time-
based alignment.
'''
# Add predictions from Isolation Forest

isolation_forest_predictions =
pd.read_csv("isolation_forest_predictions.csv")
data['IF_Anomaly'] =
isolation_forest_predictions['Anomaly_Predicted'].values

# Read reconstruction errors and anomaly predictions from
# Autoencoder results
autoencoder_results =
pd.read_csv("autoencoder_reconstruction_errors.csv",
parse_dates=["Timestamp"])
autoencoder_results.set_index("Timestamp", inplace=True)
```

```
# Merge Autoencoder results into the main dataset
data['AE_Anomaly'] = autoencoder_results['Anomaly_Predicted']
data['Reconstruction_Error'] =
autoencoder_results['Reconstruction_Error']

'''

Isolation Forest Predictions:
Adds anomaly predictions from isolation_forest_predictions.csv to
the dataset as IF_Anomaly.
Autoencoder Predictions:
Reads autoencoder_reconstruction_errors.csv to integrate AE_Anomaly
and Reconstruction_Error into the dataset.
'''
# Threshold handling
if 'Threshold' in autoencoder_results.columns:
    threshold = autoencoder_results['Threshold'].iloc[0]
else:
    threshold =
autoencoder_results['Reconstruction_Error'].quantile(0.95)  #
Calculate threshold dynamically

'''

Checks for a Threshold column in the Autoencoder results file:
If present, it uses the provided value.
Otherwise, calculates the threshold dynamically as the 95th
percentile of the reconstruction errors.
'''


# Plot 1: System Metrics with Anomalies Detected by Isolation
Forest
'''
Objective: Highlight anomalies detected by Isolation Forest in the
CPU_Usage metric.
Red Points: Indicate timestamps flagged as anomalies.
'''
plt.figure(figsize=(12, 6))
plt.plot(data.index, data['CPU_Usage'], label='CPU Usage',
color='blue', alpha=0.7)
plt.scatter(
    data.index[data['IF_Anomaly'] == 1],
    data['CPU_Usage'][data['IF_Anomaly'] == 1],
    color='red',
    label='Isolation Forest Anomalies'
)
plt.title("CPU Usage with Anomalies Detected by Isolation Forest")
plt.xlabel("Timestamp")
plt.ylabel("CPU Usage (%)")
plt.legend()
```

```
plt.grid()
plt.show()

# Plot 2: System Metrics with Anomalies Detected by Autoencoder
# Objective: Similar to Plot 1, but visualizes anomalies detected
by the Autoencoder.
plt.figure(figsize=(12, 6))
plt.plot(data.index, data['CPU_Usage'], label='CPU Usage',
color='blue', alpha=0.7)
plt.scatter(
    data.index[data['AE_Anomaly'] == 1],
    data['CPU_Usage'][data['AE_Anomaly'] == 1],
    color='orange',
    label='Autoencoder Anomalies'
)
plt.title("CPU Usage with Anomalies Detected by Autoencoder")
plt.xlabel("Timestamp")
plt.ylabel("CPU Usage (%)")
plt.legend()
plt.grid()
plt.show()

# Plot 3: Reconstruction Errors from Autoencoder
'''
Objective: Show reconstruction errors over time.
Red Dashed Line: Represents the threshold. Points above this line
are anomalies.
'''
plt.figure(figsize=(12, 6))
plt.plot(autoencoder_results.index,
autoencoder_results['Reconstruction_Error'], label='Reconstruction
Error', color='green')
plt.axhline(y=threshold, color='red', linestyle='--',
label='Threshold')
plt.title("Reconstruction Errors for Autoencoder")
plt.xlabel("Timestamp")
plt.ylabel("Reconstruction Error")
plt.legend()
plt.grid()
plt.show()

# Plot 4: Comparison of Anomaly Counts
'''
Objective: Compare the total anomalies detected by each model.
Bar Chart:
Height of bars indicates the number of anomalies detected.
Red for Isolation Forest, Orange for Autoencoder.
'''
```

```
anomaly_counts = {
    "Isolation Forest": data['IF_Anomaly'].sum(),
    "Autoencoder": data['AE_Anomaly'].sum()
}
plt.figure(figsize=(8, 6))
plt.bar(anomaly_counts.keys(), anomaly_counts.values(),
color=['red', 'orange'])
plt.title("Comparison of Anomaly Counts Detected by Models")
plt.ylabel("Number of Anomalies")
plt.grid(axis='y')
plt.show()
```

Description of Visualizations

1. **System Metrics with Anomalies**:
   - Isolation Forest:
     - Highlights anomalies detected by the Isolation Forest model on the CPU_Usage metric.
     - Red points indicate anomalies, showing significant spikes or irregular patterns.
   - Autoencoder:
     - Similar plot with anomalies detected by the Autoencoder model.
     - Orange points represent anomalies, focusing on subtle irregularities.
2. **Reconstruction Errors from Autoencoder**:
   - Plots the reconstruction errors for each data point.
   - A red dashed line represents the anomaly detection threshold.
   - Points above the threshold are flagged as anomalies, providing insight into the Autoencoder's detection mechanism.
3. **Comparison of Anomaly Counts**:
   - Bar chart comparing the total number of anomalies detected by each model.
   - Helps evaluate which model is more sensitive or conservative in detecting anomalies.

Insights from Visualizations

1. **Isolation Forest Performance**:
   - Captures prominent anomalies, especially spikes in metrics.
   - May miss subtle irregularities due to its reliance on recursive partitioning.

2. **Autoencoder Performance**:
   o Effectively identifies subtle anomalies through reconstruction errors.
   o May flag more anomalies compared to Isolation Forest due to its sensitivity.

3. **Model Comparison**:
   o The bar chart shows differences in anomaly detection counts, enabling teams to decide which model aligns better with their operational goals.

Visualizing anomalies and comparing model performance provides a clear understanding of how different algorithms detect irregularities. These insights help IT operations teams select the most effective model for their specific use cases. By integrating these visualizations into dashboards, teams can monitor system health, detect issues early, and take proactive measures to ensure reliability.

3.8 Evaluating Anomaly Detection Models

Evaluating anomaly detection models is a crucial step in determining their effectiveness and applicability to real-world scenarios. This process involves assessing the performance of models such as Isolation Forest and Autoencoder against key metrics to ensure their predictions align with operational needs. By thoroughly evaluating these models, organizations can identify their strengths and limitations, leading to better-informed decisions for anomaly detection in IT operations.

Importance of Model Evaluation

Anomaly detection is not just about flagging anomalies; it is about doing so accurately and reliably. False positives (normal instances classified as anomalies) can lead to unnecessary resource allocation, while false negatives (anomalies classified as normal) can result in undetected critical issues. Therefore, evaluating models is essential to balance precision, recall, and overall efficiency in detecting anomalies.

Key Evaluation Metrics
1. **Accuracy**:
   o Measures the percentage of correctly identified anomalies and normal instances.

  o Useful when the dataset has a balanced distribution of anomalies and normal instances.

Formula:

$$\text{Accuracy} = \frac{\text{True Positives} + \text{True Negatives}}{\text{Total Instances}}$$

2. **Precision:**
  o Indicates the proportion of predicted anomalies that are actual anomalies.
  o High precision minimizes false alarms.

Formula:

$$\text{Precision} = \frac{\text{True Positives}}{\text{True Positives} + \text{False Positives}}$$

3. **Recall (Sensitivity):**
  o Measures the proportion of actual anomalies that were correctly identified.
  o High recall ensures critical issues are not missed.

Formula:

$$\text{Recall} = \frac{\text{True Positives}}{\text{True Positives} + \text{False Negatives}}$$

4. **F1 Score:**
  o Harmonic mean of precision and recall.
  o Provides a balanced measure of a model's performance, especially when the class distribution is imbalanced.

Formula:

$$\text{F1 Score} = 2 \times \frac{\text{Precision} \times \text{Recall}}{\text{Precision} + \text{Recall}}$$

5. **ROC-AUC (Receiver Operating Characteristic - Area Under Curve):**
  o Assesses the model's ability to distinguish between normal and anomalous instances.
  o A higher AUC indicates better discrimination.

6. **Execution Time:**
  o Measures the time taken by the model to detect anomalies.
  o Important for real-time monitoring scenarios where speed is critical.

Comparison of Isolation Forest and Autoencoder

ISOLATION FOREST	AUTOENCODER
Strengths:	
• Efficient with high-dimensional data. • Works well with unlabeled data. • Minimal preprocessing required.	• Can capture complex relationships in data using reconstruction errors. • Customizable architecture for specific datasets.
Limitations:	
• May struggle with subtle anomalies or when the dataset is small	• Requires labeled data for threshold determination. • Computationally intensive compared to Isolation Forest.

Steps to Evaluate Models

1. **Data Preparation:**
   - o Split the dataset into training and testing subsets.
   - o Ensure the testing dataset includes both normal and anomalous data.
2. **Model Training and Prediction:**
   - o Train Isolation Forest on normal instances and predict anomalies.
   - o Train Autoencoder on normal data and compute reconstruction errors for testing data.
3. **Threshold Determination:**
   - o Use domain knowledge or percentile-based thresholds for each model to classify anomalies.
4. **Calculate Metrics:**
   - o Compute accuracy, precision, recall, F1 score, and AUC for both models.
   - o Measure execution time for both training and prediction phases.

Visualization of Evaluation Results

```
from sklearn.metrics import classification_report, roc_auc_score,
confusion_matrix
```

```python
import seaborn as sns
import matplotlib.pyplot as plt
import pandas as pd

# Load the main dataset
data = pd.read_csv("anomaly_detection_data.csv",
parse_dates=["Timestamp"])
data.set_index("Timestamp", inplace=True)
autoencoder_results =
pd.read_csv("autoencoder_reconstruction_errors.csv",
parse_dates=["Timestamp"])
autoencoder_results.set_index("Timestamp", inplace=True)
data['AE_Anomaly'] = autoencoder_results['Anomaly_Predicted']

isolation_forest_predictions =
pd.read_csv("isolation_forest_predictions.csv")
data['IF_Anomaly'] =
isolation_forest_predictions['Anomaly_Predicted'].values

# Evaluate Isolation Forest
if_y_true = data['Anomaly']
if_y_pred = data['IF_Anomaly']
if_auc = roc_auc_score(if_y_true, if_y_pred)
print("Isolation Forest Evaluation:")
print(classification_report(if_y_true, if_y_pred))
print(f"AUC Score: {if_auc}")

# Confusion Matrix for Isolation Forest
if_cm = confusion_matrix(if_y_true, if_y_pred)
sns.heatmap(if_cm, annot=True, fmt='d', cmap='Blues',
xticklabels=["Normal", "Anomalous"], yticklabels=["Normal",
"Anomalous"])
plt.title("Confusion Matrix - Isolation Forest")
plt.xlabel("Predicted")
plt.ylabel("Actual")
plt.show()

# Evaluate Autoencoder
ae_y_true = data['Anomaly']
ae_y_pred = data['AE_Anomaly']
ae_auc = roc_auc_score(ae_y_true, ae_y_pred)
print("Autoencoder Evaluation:")
print(classification_report(ae_y_true, ae_y_pred))
print(f"AUC Score: {ae_auc}")

# Confusion Matrix for Autoencoder
ae_cm = confusion_matrix(ae_y_true, ae_y_pred)
sns.heatmap(ae_cm, annot=True, fmt='d', cmap='Oranges',
```

```
xticklabels=["Normal", "Anomalous"], yticklabels=["Normal",
"Anomalous"])
plt.title("Confusion Matrix - Autoencoder")
plt.xlabel("Predicted")
plt.ylabel("Actual")
plt.show()
```

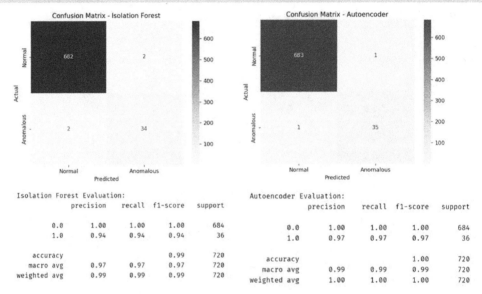

Figure 3: Sample output from model evaluation code

- **Confusion Matrix**:
  - o Illustrates the true positives, true negatives, false positives, and false negatives for each model.
- **ROC Curve**:
  - o Plots the true positive rate (TPR) against the false positive rate (FPR) at various threshold settings.
- **Bar Chart**:
  - o Compare metrics such as F1 score and precision between models.
- **Execution Time Comparison**:
  - o Line or bar charts to highlight the computational efficiency of each model.

3.9 Challenges in Real-Time Anomaly Detection

Real-time anomaly detection is a powerful tool for proactive IT management, but it comes with its own set of challenges. By understanding these challenges and adopting best practices, organizations can build robust anomaly detection systems that enhance system reliability, reduce downtime, and ensure seamless operations.

Addressing these challenges head-on will enable organizations to harness the full potential of real-time monitoring and anomaly detection.

1. Data Volume and Velocity: In a real-time setting, systems generate vast amounts of data at high velocity.
- Key Challenges:
    - Scalability: Ensuring that the anomaly detection system can handle increasing data volumes without performance degradation.
    - Latency: Detecting anomalies with minimal delay to allow for timely interventions.
- Example: A data center monitoring CPU, memory, and network usage for thousands of servers may struggle to process all incoming data streams in real time, leading to delayed or missed anomaly detection.

2. Defining Anomalies: The concept of an anomaly is often context-specific and can vary across different systems and use cases. What is considered anomalous in one environment might be normal in another.
- Key Challenges:
    - Contextual Anomalies: Anomalies that depend on specific conditions, such as time of day or workload patterns.
    - Dynamic Thresholds: Static thresholds for anomaly detection may not capture the nuances of fluctuating system behavior.
- Example: A spike in network latency during a system backup might be normal, while the same spike during regular operations could indicate an issue. Static thresholds might fail to differentiate between these scenarios.

3. Noise in Data: System metrics often contain noise, making it difficult to distinguish between normal fluctuations and genuine anomalies. High noise levels can lead to false positives or false negatives, undermining the effectiveness of the anomaly detection system.
- Key Challenges:
    - False Positives: Frequent alerts for non-issues can lead to alert fatigue, causing operators to overlook critical anomalies.
    - False Negatives: Failure to detect true anomalies can result in undiagnosed issues escalating into critical problems.
- Example: A slight variation in disk I/O rates might trigger an anomaly alert in a noisy dataset, even though the system is functioning normally.

4. Computational Resource Constraints: Real-time anomaly detection involves continuous monitoring and processing of data streams, which can be resource-intensive. High-dimensional data and complex algorithms, such as neural networks or clustering methods, further exacerbate resource constraints.

- Key Challenges:
  - Hardware Limitations: Limited CPU, memory, and storage resources can bottleneck real-time analysis.
  - Algorithm Efficiency: Balancing model accuracy and computational efficiency is difficult, especially in resource-constrained environments.
- Example: Deploying an autoencoder-based anomaly detection model on edge devices with limited hardware capabilities might result in slower performance and increased latency.

5. Lack of Labeled Data: Anomaly detection often relies on supervised or semi-supervised learning techniques, which require labeled datasets for training. However, obtaining labeled data for anomalies is challenging due to their rarity and diversity.

- Key Challenges:
  - Imbalanced Data: Anomalies are rare events, leading to datasets dominated by normal instances.
  - Annotation Effort: Labeling anomalies requires domain expertise and significant manual effort.
- Example: A network security system may struggle to identify anomalies accurately without labeled data representing past cyberattacks.

6. Real-Time Model Adaptation: System behaviors change over time due to software updates, hardware upgrades, and evolving user patterns. Anomaly detection models must adapt to these changes to remain effective.

- Key Challenges:
  - Concept Drift: The statistical properties of the data change over time, rendering previously trained models obsolete.
  - Continuous Learning: Updating models in real time without interrupting system operations is difficult.
- Example: A cloud infrastructure's network traffic patterns might change after scaling up its resources, requiring the anomaly detection model to adjust its baseline.

7. Integration with IT Systems: Anomaly detection systems must seamlessly integrate with existing IT operations and monitoring tools to provide actionable insights. However, this integration often involves technical and organizational challenges.

- Key Challenges:
    - o Compatibility: Ensuring compatibility with diverse data sources and IT environments.
    - o Actionable Insights: Translating raw anomaly detections into meaningful insights for IT teams.
- Example: Integrating an anomaly detection system with a legacy monitoring tool might require custom data pipelines and APIs, increasing implementation complexity.

8. Privacy and Security Concerns: In environments where sensitive data is being monitored, privacy and security concerns can limit the scope and capabilities of anomaly detection systems.

- Key Challenges:
    - o Data Privacy: Protecting sensitive data while enabling effective anomaly detection.
    - o Data Encryption: Ensuring secure transmission and storage of monitored data.
- Example: A healthcare IT system monitoring patient data must comply with strict privacy regulations, which might restrict the types of data that can be analyzed.

Best Practices to Address Challenges
1. **Use Scalable Architectures**:
    - o Implement distributed processing frameworks like Apache Kafka or Apache Flink to handle high data volumes.
2. **Adopt Context-Aware Models**:
    - o Use dynamic thresholds or contextual anomaly detection models to account for varying conditions.
3. **Denoise Data**:
    - o Apply data preprocessing techniques like smoothing or filtering to reduce noise.
4. **Optimize Computational Efficiency**:
    - o Use lightweight models or approximate methods for real-time applications.
5. **Leverage Unsupervised Learning**:

  o Use algorithms like Isolation Forest or clustering methods that do not require labeled data.

6. **Implement Continuous Monitoring**:
  o Use adaptive learning techniques to keep models updated with changing system behaviors.

7. **Ensure Seamless Integration**:
  o Design modular systems that can easily integrate with existing IT tools and workflows.

8. **Prioritize Data Security**:
  o Encrypt data and anonymize sensitive information to comply with privacy regulations.

3.10 Conclusion

Real-time anomaly detection has become a cornerstone of modern IT operations, enabling organizations to proactively identify and resolve issues before they escalate into critical problems. By leveraging advanced Machine Learning techniques and integrating them with real-time monitoring systems, businesses can enhance operational efficiency, reduce downtime, and improve overall system reliability. This chapter explored the methodologies, challenges, and best practices in implementing real-time anomaly detection, and it's now time to tie these insights together while highlighting the real-world applications of these systems.

Real-World Applications of Anomaly Detection

1. IT Infrastructure Monitoring

- **Application**: Monitoring servers, networks, and databases to detect unusual patterns in system metrics like CPU usage, memory consumption, and network latency.
- **Impact**:
  o Early detection of potential hardware failures.
  o Prevention of system outages through proactive maintenance.
- **Example**: A data center uses real-time anomaly detection to identify abnormal spikes in network latency, preventing a server crash caused by unexpected traffic.

2. Cybersecurity

- **Application**: Identifying suspicious activities, such as unauthorized access or unusual data transfers, to safeguard systems against cyber threats.
- **Impact**:
  o Mitigation of potential security breaches.

- o Protection of sensitive data and system integrity.
- **Example**: A financial institution employs anomaly detection to monitor login attempts, flagging unusual patterns indicative of a brute-force attack.

3. E-Commerce and Retail Operations
- **Application**: Tracking inventory levels, customer transactions, and website traffic to identify anomalies that may indicate fraudulent activity or system inefficiencies.
- **Impact**:
  - o Improved customer experience through system reliability.
  - o Prevention of revenue losses due to fraud or stock mismanagement.
- **Example**: An e-commerce platform detects unusual spikes in failed transactions, leading to the identification of a payment gateway issue.

4. Manufacturing and IoT
- **Application**: Monitoring IoT devices, production lines, and machinery to detect deviations from normal operating conditions.
- **Impact**:
  - o Reduction in unplanned downtime and maintenance costs.
  - o Optimization of production processes.
- **Example**: A manufacturing plant uses anomaly detection to identify early signs of wear and tear in assembly line equipment, preventing costly breakdowns.

5. Healthcare
- **Application**: Monitoring patient health data in real time to identify anomalies in vital signs or medical device performance.
- **Impact**:
  - o Enhanced patient care through early intervention.
  - o Prevention of critical health emergencies.
- **Example**: A hospital implements anomaly detection to monitor patients in the ICU, alerting staff to irregularities in heart rate or oxygen levels.

6. Financial Services
- **Application**: Detecting unusual transactions, changes in account activity, or irregularities in market data to prevent financial fraud and maintain system integrity.

- **Impact**:
  - Improved risk management.
  - Protection against monetary losses.
- **Example**: A bank employs anomaly detection to flag unusual withdrawal patterns from ATMs, uncovering a skimming operation.

7. Energy and Utilities
- **Application**: Monitoring power grids, energy consumption patterns, and equipment performance to detect potential failures or inefficiencies.
- **Impact**:
  - Minimization of power outages.
  - Optimization of energy distribution.
- **Example**: A smart grid system uses anomaly detection to identify unusual fluctuations in power usage, preventing a city-wide blackout.

Looking Forward
Real-time anomaly detection is not just a technological capability—it's a strategic advantage. As IT systems grow in complexity, the ability to detect and address anomalies in real time will become increasingly critical. The future of anomaly detection lies in:
- **Integration with AI and Automation**: Enabling autonomous systems that not only detect but also resolve issues without human intervention.
- **Scalability**: Developing models that can handle the vast data streams generated by IoT devices and cloud-based systems.
- **Explainability**: Building transparent systems that provide actionable insights alongside anomaly alerts.

Conclusion
Real-time anomaly detection represents a significant leap forward in IT operations management. By combining robust algorithms with efficient real-time processing and visualization, organizations can stay ahead of potential issues and deliver seamless, reliable services. The real-world applications discussed highlight the transformative potential of anomaly detection across industries, demonstrating its ability to enhance efficiency, security, and resilience.

As we move forward, organizations must continue to invest in innovative anomaly detection solutions, leveraging them as a foundational pillar of proactive and intelligent IT management. With the right strategies, tools, and best practices, real-time anomaly detection can become a game-changer, driving success in an increasingly data-driven world.

* * *

Root Cause Analysis
Using Log Classification

CHAPTER 4

ROOT CAUSE ANALYSIS USING LOG CLASSIFICATION

Root Cause Analysis (RCA) is a systematic process for identifying the underlying reasons behind a problem or issue. In the context of IT operations, RCA focuses on uncovering the foundational causes of system failures, performance degradations, and other operational anomalies. Understanding these causes is essential for preventing recurrence, optimizing system performance, and maintaining reliability in complex IT environments.

4.1 Introduction to Root Cause Analysis (RCA)

Root Cause Analysis is not just about addressing the symptoms of a problem; it is about drilling down to the core issue. By systematically investigating the sequence of events leading to an issue, RCA provides a structured approach to identify the root cause. This ensures that corrective actions target the source of the problem rather than merely treating its symptoms.

For instance, a system downtime might initially seem like a network connectivity issue, but RCA could reveal that it was triggered by a misconfigured router or outdated firmware.

Importance of RCA in IT Operations

In IT environments, where systems are increasingly complex and interconnected, even minor issues can cascade into significant problems. Effective RCA offers several benefits:

1. **Prevention of Recurring Issues**: By identifying and addressing the root cause, RCA helps prevent similar issues from reoccurring, saving time and resources.
2. **Improved System Reliability**: RCA enhances the stability and reliability of IT systems by resolving foundational issues that may compromise performance.
3. **Optimized Resource Allocation**: With RCA, IT teams can focus their efforts on resolving critical issues rather than repeatedly addressing surface-level symptoms.

4. **Enhanced Decision-Making**: RCA provides actionable insights that inform strategic decisions, such as system upgrades, resource allocation, or process redesign.

Why Automate Root Cause Analysis?

Traditional RCA methods often involve manual analysis of system logs, interviews with stakeholders, and iterative troubleshooting. While effective in small-scale systems, manual RCA becomes impractical in large, dynamic IT environments.

Automation of RCA, particularly through Machine Learning techniques, addresses several challenges:

- **Scalability**: Automated tools can process large volumes of data in real time, enabling RCA in complex environments.
- **Speed**: Automation reduces the time needed to identify root causes, minimizing downtime and associated costs.
- **Accuracy**: Machine Learning models analyze patterns and correlations in data, uncovering root causes that might be overlooked by manual methods.

For example, an automated RCA system could analyze millions of log entries in seconds, pinpointing the exact configuration error that caused a server outage.

Challenges of Manual RCA

Manual RCA faces several limitations in modern IT environments:

- **Data Volume**: The sheer volume of system logs and metrics makes manual analysis time-consuming and error-prone.
- **Complex Interdependencies**: IT systems often involve intricate interdependencies, making it difficult to trace issues back to their root causes.
- **Human Error**: Manual analysis is susceptible to biases and oversights, which can lead to incorrect conclusions.

These challenges underscore the need for automated approaches to RCA, which can handle the complexity and scale of modern IT systems.

How Log Classification Aids RCA

Log classification is a powerful technique that uses Machine Learning algorithms to automate the identification of root causes in system logs. By categorizing log entries based on labeled outcomes (e.g. "network failure," "disk failure"), log classification models can quickly and accurately pinpoint the underlying issue.

For example:
- A log entry with an error code indicating high disk usage could be classified as "disk failure."
- Another entry with repeated timeout errors might be labeled as "network congestion."

These classifications enable IT teams to focus their efforts on resolving the root cause, rather than sifting through logs manually.

Setting the Stage for Automated RCA

This chapter will delve into how supervised learning algorithms, such as Logistic Regression and Random Forest, can be used to classify logs and automate the RCA process. By the end of this chapter, you will understand:
- The importance of RCA in IT operations.
- The challenges of manual RCA and the benefits of automation.
- How to leverage Machine Learning techniques to classify logs and identify root causes efficiently.

By integrating these techniques into IT workflows, organizations can transform their approach to problem-solving, achieving faster resolutions and more reliable systems. This shift to data-driven RCA marks a significant step forward in IT operations management, paving the way for smarter and more proactive operational strategies.

4.2 Understanding System Logs

System logs are the lifeblood of IT operations management. They serve as a comprehensive record of system activities, capturing everything from routine events to critical errors. For IT professionals, system logs are invaluable resources for diagnosing issues, monitoring performance, and conducting root cause analysis (RCA). Understanding the structure, significance, and challenges associated with system logs is essential for leveraging them effectively, especially in Machine Learning-driven log classification.

What Are System Logs?

System logs are chronological records generated by software applications, operating systems, servers, and network devices. They document system activities, events, and processes, providing a detailed trail of operations that can be analyzed for insights.

Examples of System Logs:
- **Application Logs**: Record events specific to a software application, such as user interactions or error messages.
- **System Logs**: Capture operating system-level activities, including boot processes, system errors, and hardware interactions.
- **Network Logs**: Document network activities like connection requests, traffic patterns, and failed logins.
- **Security Logs**: Focus on security-related events, such as unauthorized access attempts or policy violations.

Why Are System Logs Important?
System logs play a pivotal role in maintaining the health and performance of IT environments. Their importance lies in the following areas:

1. **Issue Diagnosis**:
   - Logs provide detailed error messages and timestamps that help IT teams identify and resolve system failures.
2. **Performance Monitoring**:
   - Metrics like CPU usage, memory consumption, and network latency can be extracted from logs to monitor system performance.
3. **Security Auditing**:
   - Logs help track security breaches, detect anomalies, and ensure compliance with regulations.
4. **Predictive Maintenance**:
   - Historical log data can be analyzed to predict potential failures and schedule proactive maintenance.

Structure of System Logs
System logs are typically semi-structured or unstructured, making them challenging to process directly. A typical log entry consists of the following components:

1. **Timestamp**:
   - Indicates when the event occurred, enabling chronological analysis.
   - Example: 2024-12-25 14:32:45
2. **Log Level**:
   - Specifies the severity of the event, such as INFO, DEBUG, WARNING, or ERROR.
   - Example: [ERROR]

3. **Source**:
   - o Identifies the application, service, or component that generated the log.
   - o Example: DatabaseService

4. **Message**:
   - o Describes the event, often including error codes or diagnostic details.
   - o Example: Connection timed out after 30 seconds

5. **Additional Metadata**:
   - o May include IP addresses, user IDs, or transaction IDs for more context.
   - o Example: UserID: 12345, IP: 192.168.1.1

Challenges in Working with System Logs

1. **Volume**:
   - o Modern IT environments generate an overwhelming amount of log data. Managing and analyzing this data in real time is a significant challenge.

2. **Noise**:
   - o Logs often contain redundant or irrelevant information, making it difficult to focus on actionable insights.

3. **Inconsistency**:
   - o Log formats can vary across systems and applications, requiring extensive preprocessing to standardize the data.

4. **Unstructured Data**:
   - o Logs are frequently written in natural language or a mix of structured and unstructured formats, complicating automated analysis.

5. **Dynamic Nature**:
   - o As systems evolve, the types of events and log formats can change, requiring flexible and adaptive solutions.

Preparing System Logs for Machine Learning

To use system logs effectively in supervised learning, it's essential to preprocess and structure the data. The following steps are commonly involved:

1. **Parsing and Tokenization**:
   - o Extract meaningful components (e.g. timestamp, message) from raw logs using tools like regular expressions or log parsers.

2. **Feature Engineering**:
   o Convert text-based log entries into numerical representations suitable for Machine Learning. Examples include:
     ▪ One-hot encoding for categorical features (e.g. log levels).
     ▪ Natural language processing (NLP) techniques for log messages.
3. **Labeling Data**:
   o Assign labels to log entries based on known outcomes (e.g. "network failure" or "disk failure"). This step is crucial for supervised learning.
4. **Handling Imbalanced Data**:
   o Anomalies are often rare in log data. Techniques like oversampling, undersampling, or using weighted loss functions can address this imbalance.

Example of a Log Entry and Its Components

Consider the following sample log entry:

```
2024-12-25 14:32:45 [ERROR] DatabaseService - Connection
timed out after 30 seconds
```

Components:
- **Timestamp**: 2024-12-25 14:32:45
- **Log Level**: [ERROR]
- **Source**: DatabaseService
- **Message**: Connection timed out after 30 seconds

Feature Extraction for Machine Learning:
- **Log Level (Categorical)**: [ERROR] → Encoded as [0, 0, 1, 0] (assuming INFO, DEBUG, ERROR, CRITICAL)
- **Message (Text)**: NLP techniques like TF-IDF or word embeddings to capture semantic information.

Using System Logs for Root Cause Analysis

By analyzing system logs with Machine Learning models, IT teams can automate the process of root cause identification. For example:
- A classifier trained on labeled log data can categorize logs into predefined root causes.

- Logs labeled as "network failure" might point to configuration issues or hardware problems in the network infrastructure.

4.3 Data Preparation for Log Classification

Steps in Data Preparation for Log Classification

Step 1: Data Collection

System logs are collected from various sources, such as:

- Application logs.
- System logs.
- Network logs.
- Security logs.

Logs are usually stored in text files, JSON, or databases. Ensure that the data collected is relevant to the classification task, such as logs containing labeled outcomes like "network failure" or "disk failure."

```
2024-12-25 14:32:45 [ERROR] NetworkService - Connection timed out after
30 seconds 2024-12-25 14:35:12 [INFO] DiskService - Disk usage at 80%
```

Step 2: Data Cleaning

Raw logs often include redundant, irrelevant, or erroneous data. Cleaning involves:

1. **Removing Duplicates**:
   o Identify and remove duplicate log entries to avoid biased training.
2. **Handling Missing Data**:
   o Fill missing values with placeholders or drop incomplete entries, depending on their relevance.
3. **Standardizing Log Formats**:
   o Ensure consistent date formats, log levels, and field delimiters.

Step 3: Parsing and Structuring Logs

Logs are often semi-structured or unstructured. Parsing extracts relevant fields and converts logs into a structured format, such as a DataFrame.

Example: From this log entry:

```
2024-12-25 14:32:45 [ERROR] NetworkService - Connection timed out after 30
seconds
```

Extract the following fields:

- **Timestamp**: 2024-12-25 14:32:45

- **Log Level**: [ERROR]
- **Service**: NetworkService
- **Message**: Connection timed out after 30 seconds

```python
import re
import pandas as pd

data = pd.read_csv("log_classification_dataset.csv")
# Define regex for parsing
log_pattern = r"(?P<Timestamp>\d+-\d+-\d+ \d+:\d+:\d+)
\[(?P<LogLevel>\w+)\] (?P<Service>\w+) - (?P<Message>.+)"
parsed_logs = data['LogLevel'].str.extract(log_pattern)

# Combine with original dataset
data = pd.concat([data, parsed_logs], axis=1)
print(data)
```

Step 4: Feature Engineering

Feature engineering transforms raw log data into features that Machine Learning models can use effectively.

1. **Encoding Log Levels**:
   - Convert categorical values like [INFO], [ERROR], etc., into numerical representations.
   - Example: INFO=0, ERROR=1.
2. **Text Feature Extraction**:
   - Use natural language processing (NLP) techniques to analyze log messages.
   - Convert text to numerical features using techniques like TF-IDF or word embeddings.

```python
from sklearn.feature_extraction.text import TfidfVectorizer

# Extract features from log messages
vectorizer = TfidfVectorizer(max_features=100)
message_features =
vectorizer.fit_transform(data['Message']).toarray()
```

3. **Timestamp Features**:
- Derive features like the time of day, day of the week, or elapsed time between events.

```
data['Hour'] = pd.to_datetime(data['Timestamp']).dt.hour
data['DayOfWeek'] = pd.to_datetime(data['Timestamp']).dt.dayofweek
```

Step 5: Labeling Data

For supervised learning, logs must be labeled with their respective outcomes (e.g. "network failure," "disk failure"). Labels can be:
- Manually assigned by domain experts.
- Automatically inferred using predefined rules or heuristics.

```
# Assign labels based on error keywords
data['Label'] = data['Message'].apply(lambda x: "network failure" if
"Connection timed out" in x else "disk failure")
```

Step 6: Splitting Data into Training and Testing Sets

Split the dataset into training and testing sets to evaluate model performance.

```
from sklearn.model_selection import train_test_split

# Split data
X = data[['LogLevel', 'Hour', 'DayOfWeek', 'Message_Features']]
y = data['Label']
X_train, X_test, y_train, y_test = train_test_split(X, y,
test_size=0.2, random_state=1)
```

Overcoming Common Challenges
1. **Handling Unstructured Data**:
   o Logs often contain free-form text, which requires careful parsing and NLP techniques for effective analysis.
2. **Imbalanced Data**:
   o Anomalous events are rare, leading to imbalanced datasets. Use techniques like oversampling, undersampling, or class-weighted models to address this.
3. **Large-Scale Data**:
   o Large volumes of log data require efficient preprocessing tools like Apache Spark or Dask for scalability.

4.4 Introduction to Log Classification Algorithms

System logs, generated continuously across various components of IT infrastructure, contain critical information about system activities, performance, and failures. However, manually analyzing these logs is labor-intensive, error-prone, and time-consuming. Log classification offers a structured approach to process and categorize logs, enabling faster and more accurate insights.

For example:

- A network-related error log can be classified under "network failure," prompting IT teams to investigate network components.
- Logs related to storage issues can be categorized as "disk failure," narrowing the scope of investigation.

By automating this process, log classification helps:

1. **Improve Incident Response Time**: Quickly identifying the root cause reduces downtime and enhances system reliability.
2. **Enable Proactive Maintenance**: Patterns in classified logs can reveal early signs of potential failures, enabling preventive action.
3. **Enhance Resource Allocation**: Categorizing logs based on severity and impact helps prioritize resources effectively.

Selecting the Right Algorithm

Choosing the right algorithm depends on several factors, including:

- **Nature of the Data**: For structured logs, traditional algorithms like Logistic Regression or Random Forest may suffice. For unstructured text logs, Neural Networks or Naive Bayes are better suited.
- **Complexity of the Problem**: For simple binary classification, Logistic Regression is ideal. For complex, multi-class problems, Random Forest or SVM may be more effective.
- **Data Volume**: Large datasets require algorithms that scale well, like Random Forest or Neural Networks.
- **Interpretability**: If explainability is critical, Logistic Regression or Random Forest is preferable over Neural Networks.

Example Scenario: Using Random Forest for Log Classification

Objective: Classify logs into categories such as "network failure," "disk failure," and "authentication failure."

Approach:

1. Preprocess logs to extract features like log level, service, and error keywords.
2. Train a Random Forest model on labeled log data.

3. Evaluate model performance using metrics like accuracy, precision, and recall.
4. Deploy the model to classify incoming logs in real time.

4.5 Implementing Log Classification with Logistic Regression

Logistic Regression is a simple yet powerful supervised learning algorithm used for classification tasks. Its ability to predict probabilities for binary or multi-class outcomes makes it an excellent choice for classifying system logs into predefined categories such as "network failure," "disk failure," or "authentication failure."

In this section, we will implement Logistic Regression using the log_classification_dataset.csv file, which contains structured log data. The process will involve data preprocessing, feature engineering, model training, and evaluation.

Problem Statement

The objective is to classify system logs into categories (e.g. "network failure," "disk failure") based on features like LogLevel, Service, and Message. This classification will automate root cause analysis, enabling IT teams to quickly identify and resolve system issues.

Step-by-Step Implementation

Step 1: Load and Inspect the Dataset

The first step is to load the dataset and explore its structure.

```
import pandas as pd

# Load the dataset
data = pd.read_csv("log_classification_dataset.csv")

# Display the first few rows of the dataset
print(data.head())
```

Dataset Columns:
- **Timestamp:** The date and time of the log entry.
- **LogLevel:** The severity level of the log (e.g. INFO, WARNING, ERROR).
- **Service:** The source service generating the log (e.g. NetworkService, DiskService).

- **Message**: The description of the log event.
- **Label**: The target variable indicating the log category (e.g. network failure, disk failure).

Step 2: Preprocess the Data

To train the Logistic Regression model, we must convert categorical features into numerical representations and preprocess the text data.

```python
from sklearn.feature_extraction.text import TfidfVectorizer
from sklearn.preprocessing import LabelEncoder

# Encode LogLevel and Service as numerical features
data['LogLevel'] = LabelEncoder().fit_transform(data['LogLevel'])
data['Service'] = LabelEncoder().fit_transform(data['Service'])

# Convert the 'Message' column into numerical features using TF-IDF
vectorizer = TfidfVectorizer(max_features=100)
message_features =
vectorizer.fit_transform(data['Message']).toarray()

# Combine all features into a single DataFrame
features = pd.concat([
    data[['LogLevel', 'Service']],
    pd.DataFrame(message_features,
columns=vectorizer.get_feature_names_out())
], axis=1)

# Encode the target variable (Label)
labels = LabelEncoder().fit_transform(data['Label'])
```

Step 3: Split the Data

Split the dataset into training and testing sets to evaluate the model.

```python
from sklearn.model_selection import train_test_split

# Split data into training and testing sets
X_train, X_test, y_train, y_test = train_test_split(features,
labels, test_size=0.2, random_state=1)
```

Step 4: Train the Logistic Regression Model

Train the Logistic Regression model using the training data.

```
from sklearn.linear_model import LogisticRegression

# Initialize and train the Logistic Regression model
model = LogisticRegression(max_iter=500)
model.fit(X_train, y_train)
```

Step 5: Evaluate the Model
Evaluate the model's performance using metrics like accuracy, precision, and recall.

```
from sklearn.metrics import classification_report, accuracy_score

# Make predictions on the test set
y_pred = model.predict(X_test)

# Print the classification report and accuracy
print("Classification Report:")
print(classification_report(y_test, y_pred))

print("Accuracy:", accuracy_score(y_test, y_pred))
```

Step 6: Interpret Results
The model achieves an accuracy of 86%, indicating good performance in classifying logs into the target categories. The classification report provides insights into precision, recall, and F1-score for each category, highlighting areas where the model excels or requires improvement.

Step 7: Predict New Logs
Use the trained model to classify new logs and automate root cause analysis.

```
# Example new logs
new_logs = [
    {"LogLevel": "ERROR", "Service": "NetworkService", "Message":
"Connection timed out"},
    {"LogLevel": "WARNING", "Service": "DiskService", "Message":
"Disk usage at critical level"}
]

# Preprocess new logs
new_logs_df = pd.DataFrame(new_logs)
```

```
new_logs_df['LogLevel'] =
LabelEncoder().fit_transform(new_logs_df['LogLevel'])
new_logs_df['Service'] =
LabelEncoder().fit_transform(new_logs_df['Service'])
new_messages =
vectorizer.transform(new_logs_df['Message']).toarray()

# Combine features
new_features = pd.concat([
    new_logs_df[['LogLevel', 'Service']],
    pd.DataFrame(new_messages,
columns=vectorizer.get_feature_names_out())
], axis=1)

# Predict labels
predictions = model.predict(new_features)
print("Predicted Categories:", predictions)
```

Logistic Regression provides a robust and interpretable solution for log classification tasks. By preprocessing the data effectively, engineering meaningful features, and evaluating model performance, IT teams can automate root cause analysis and enhance operational efficiency. This approach ensures faster identification of issues and proactive management of IT infrastructure.

4.6 Implementing Log Classification with Random Forest

Random Forest is a robust ensemble learning algorithm widely used for classification tasks. It builds multiple decision trees during training and aggregates their outputs to improve accuracy and prevent overfitting. In this section, we will implement Random Forest using the log_classification_dataset.csv file to classify system logs into predefined categories like "network failure" or "disk failure."

Problem Statement
The objective is to classify system logs into categories such as "network failure," "disk failure," and "authentication failure" using Random Forest. This will help automate root cause analysis, enabling IT teams to address issues faster.

Steps to Solve the Problem
Step 1: Load and Inspect the Dataset
The dataset contains structured log data with the following columns:
- **Timestamp**: The date and time of the log entry.
- **LogLevel**: The severity level of the log (e.g. INFO, WARNING, ERROR).

- **Service**: The source service generating the log.
- **Message**: A description of the log event.
- **Label**: The target variable indicating the category of the log.
-

```python
import pandas as pd
# Load the dataset
data = pd.read_csv("log_classification_dataset.csv")

# Display the first few rows
print(data.head())
```

Step 2: Preprocess the Data

Convert categorical features like LogLevel, Service, and Message into numerical representations suitable for training the model.

```python
from sklearn.feature_extraction.text import TfidfVectorizer
from sklearn.preprocessing import LabelEncoder

# Encode LogLevel and Service
data['LogLevel'] = LabelEncoder().fit_transform(data['LogLevel'])
data['Service'] = LabelEncoder().fit_transform(data['Service'])

# Convert the 'Message' column into numerical features using TF-IDF
vectorizer = TfidfVectorizer(max_features=100)
message_features =
vectorizer.fit_transform(data['Message']).toarray()

# Combine all features into a single DataFrame
features = pd.concat([
    data[['LogLevel', 'Service']],
    pd.DataFrame(message_features,
columns=vectorizer.get_feature_names_out())
], axis=1)

# Encode the target variable
labels = LabelEncoder().fit_transform(data['Label'])
```

Step 3: Split the Data

Split the dataset into training and testing sets for model evaluation.

```python
from sklearn.model_selection import train_test_split
```

```
X_train, X_test, y_train, y_test = train_test_split(features,
labels, test_size=0.2, random_state=1)
```

Step 4: Train the Random Forest Model
Train a Random Forest classifier on the training data.

```python
from sklearn.ensemble import RandomForestClassifier

# Initialize and train the model
rf_model = RandomForestClassifier(n_estimators=100, random_state=42)
rf_model.fit(X_train, y_train)
```

Step 5: Evaluate the Model
Evaluate the model using metrics such as accuracy, precision, and recall.

```python
from sklearn.metrics import classification_report, accuracy_score

# Make predictions
y_pred = rf_model.predict(X_test)

# Print evaluation metrics
print("Classification Report:")
print(classification_report(y_test, y_pred))
print("Accuracy:", accuracy_score(y_test, y_pred))
```

Step 6: Classify New Logs
Predict categories for new log entries.

```python
# Example new logs
new_logs = [
    {"LogLevel": "ERROR", "Service": "NetworkService", "Message":
"Connection timed out"},
    {"LogLevel": "WARNING", "Service": "DiskService", "Message":
"Disk usage at critical level"}
]

# Preprocess new logs
new_logs_df = pd.DataFrame(new_logs)
new_logs_df['LogLevel'] =
LabelEncoder().fit_transform(new_logs_df['LogLevel'])
new_logs_df['Service'] =
LabelEncoder().fit_transform(new_logs_df['Service'])
new_messages =
```

```
vectorizer.transform(new_logs_df['Message']).toarray()

# Combine features
new_features = pd.concat([
    new_logs_df[['LogLevel', 'Service']],
    pd.DataFrame(new_messages,
columns=vectorizer.get_feature_names_out())
], axis=1)

# Predict labels for new logs
new_predictions = rf_model.predict(new_features)
print("Predicted Categories for New Logs:", new_predictions)
```

Insights and Takeaways
1. **Performance**: Random Forest achieves high accuracy and provides insights into feature importance.
2. **Interpretability**: Although less interpretable than simpler models, Random Forest's feature importance helps understand key log attributes.
3. **Deployment**: The trained model can classify incoming logs in real-time, automating root cause analysis and improving incident response time.

By leveraging Random Forest, IT teams can effectively categorize system logs, reduce manual effort, and ensure faster resolution of system issues.

4.7 Automating Root Cause Identification

Root Cause Analysis (RCA) is a critical process in IT operations management that aims to identify the underlying cause of system issues or failures. While traditional RCA methods rely on manual log inspection and human expertise, automation through Machine Learning models significantly accelerates this process, making it more efficient and accurate. Automating root cause identification allows organizations to minimize downtime, reduce costs, and enhance system reliability. This section explores the importance of automating RCA, the challenges involved, and the tools and methodologies that enable seamless implementation.

Why Automate Root Cause Identification?

1. Speed and Efficiency
In complex IT environments, systems generate massive amounts of logs every second. Manually sifting through these logs to pinpoint the root cause of an issue

is time-consuming and inefficient. Automation can process these logs in real-time, rapidly narrowing down potential causes.

2. Consistency
Manual RCA is prone to human error and inconsistencies due to varying expertise levels among analysts. Automated models provide consistent and objective analysis, ensuring reliable results every time.

3. Proactive Maintenance
By identifying patterns in logs, automated RCA tools can detect early signs of recurring issues, enabling proactive maintenance before significant failures occur.

4. Resource Optimization
Automation reduces the dependency on specialized human expertise, freeing up resources for strategic initiatives instead of reactive problem-solving.

Challenges in Automating RCA
1. **Data Quality**: Automated systems rely on high-quality data. Logs with incomplete or ambiguous entries can compromise the effectiveness of models.
2. **Complex Dependencies**: Modern IT systems often have complex interdependencies. Identifying the root cause among interconnected components requires sophisticated analysis.
3. **Dynamic Environments**: IT environments constantly evolve with new technologies and architectures. Models must adapt to these changes to remain effective.
4. **Explainability**: Automated systems must provide interpretable outputs to ensure that stakeholders trust the results and can act on them effectively.

Framework for Automating RCA
1. Data Collection and Integration
Automating RCA starts with collecting logs and metrics from various system components such as servers, networks, databases, and applications. These logs are then integrated into a centralized repository for streamlined analysis.

Example:
- Collect logs from application servers, network devices, and databases using tools like Elastic Stack or Splunk.

2. Data Preprocessing

Raw logs often contain noise or irrelevant information. Preprocessing involves cleaning, normalizing, and transforming data to ensure it is usable for Machine Learning models.

Techniques:
- Parse log entries into structured formats.
- Remove redundant or non-informative fields.
- Extract features such as error codes, timestamps, and service identifiers.

3. Feature Engineering

Feature engineering involves identifying and creating meaningful features from logs that help Machine Learning models learn patterns effectively.

Examples:
- Extract error codes, log levels, and service names as categorical features.
- Compute time-based features like the frequency of error occurrences within specific time windows.

4. Model Selection

Depending on the complexity and scale of the problem, select appropriate models for RCA. Supervised learning models such as Random Forest or Logistic Regression can classify known issues, while unsupervised models like Isolation Forest or Autoencoders can detect novel anomalies.

5. Real-Time Automation

Deploy models in a production environment to automate RCA in real-time. Logs are processed and classified as they are generated, providing immediate insights into potential root causes.

Example Implementation

Scenario: A cloud service provider wants to automate RCA for identifying root causes of service outages. Logs from network devices, databases, and application servers are analyzed using a Random Forest model.

Steps:
1. **Data Collection**: Collect logs from all service components using a log aggregation tool.
2. **Preprocessing**: Parse logs to extract features like timestamps, error messages, and log levels.
3. **Feature Engineering**: Create derived features such as error frequency, service type, and severity.

4. **Model Training**: Train a Random Forest model using labeled historical logs.
5. **Deployment**: Deploy the model in a real-time monitoring system.
6. **Visualization**: Use dashboards to display detected root causes for faster decision-making.

Outcome: When an issue occurs, the model analyzes logs in real-time and flags the most likely root cause (e.g. "Database connection timeout").

Tools and Technologies for Automated RCA

- **Log Aggregation and Processing**:
  - Tools like Splunk, Elastic Stack (ELK), or Graylog collect and preprocess logs for analysis.
- **Machine Learning Frameworks**:
  - Scikit-learn, TensorFlow, and PyTorch provide libraries for training and deploying Machine Learning models.
- **Visualization**:
  - Dashboards built using Tableau, Grafana, or Kibana help visualize RCA results for actionable insights.

Best Practices for Automating RCA

1. **Ensure Data Completeness**: Include logs from all relevant components to provide a holistic view of system behavior.
2. **Establish Thresholds for Anomalies**: Define clear thresholds for detecting anomalies to minimize false positives.
3. **Enable Feedback Loops**: Continuously refine models based on feedback from IT teams to improve accuracy.
4. **Prioritize Explainability**: Use interpretable models or supplement complex models with explainability tools to ensure trust in predictions.

4.8 Visualizing Log Classification Results

Visualization is a powerful tool for understanding and communicating the results of Machine Learning models. In the context of log classification, visualizing the outcomes helps IT teams quickly identify patterns, assess model performance, and gain actionable insights into system behavior. This section focuses on using visualizations to analyze and present the results of log classification with Random Forest.

Why Visualization is Important?

1. **Simplifies Complex Data**: Visualizations make it easier to interpret the classification of logs, especially when dealing with large datasets with thousands of log entries.
2. **Highlights Patterns and Anomalies**: Visual tools can reveal trends, such as recurring failures or spikes in specific log categories, enabling proactive issue resolution.
3. **Supports Decision-Making**: Clear visuals help IT teams prioritize actions based on the severity or frequency of classified issues.

Key Visualization Goals

1. **Category Distribution**: Show the distribution of classified log categories, such as "network failure," "disk failure," etc., to highlight prevalent issues.
2. **Model Performance Metrics**: Illustrate accuracy, precision, recall, and F1-score to evaluate the model's effectiveness.
3. **Comparison of Predicted vs. Actual Labels**: Use confusion matrices or bar charts to compare the predicted labels against the true labels.
4. **Feature Importance**: Highlight the most influential features in the Random Forest model to understand what drives predictions.

Example Visualizations

1. Distribution of Classified Logs

A bar chart showing the count of logs in each category provides a high-level overview of system issues.

```python
import matplotlib.pyplot as plt
import pandas as pd
import numpy as np

# Count the occurrences of each predicted class
class_counts = pd.Series(y_pred).value_counts()
#class_labels =
LabelEncoder().inverse_transform(class_counts.index)
class_labels = LabelEncoder().fit_transform(class_counts.index)

plt.figure(figsize=(8, 6))
plt.bar(class_labels, class_counts.values, color='skyblue')
plt.title("Distribution of Classified Logs")
plt.xlabel("Log Categories")
plt.ylabel("Count")
plt.grid(axis='y')
plt.show()
```

2. Confusion Matrix

A confusion matrix visually represents the performance of the classifier by showing the true positives, false positives, and false negatives for each class.

```python
from sklearn.metrics import ConfusionMatrixDisplay

ConfusionMatrixDisplay.from_predictions(y_test, y_pred,
display_labels=LabelEncoder().fit_transform(np.unique(labels)))
plt.title("Confusion Matrix")
plt.show()
```

3. Feature Importance

Random Forest provides a feature importance metric, which indicates the relative contribution of each feature to the model's decisions.

```python
# Extract feature importance
feature_importances = rf_model.feature_importances_
feature_names = features.columns

# Plot feature importance
plt.figure(figsize=(10, 6))
plt.barh(feature_names, feature_importances, color='lightgreen')
plt.title("Feature Importance in Log Classification")
plt.xlabel("Importance Score")
plt.ylabel("Features")
plt.grid(axis='x')
plt.show()
```

4. Comparison of Actual vs. Predicted Counts

A side-by-side bar chart compares the count of actual and predicted labels for each category.

```python
actual_counts = pd.Series(y_test).value_counts()
predicted_counts = pd.Series(y_pred).value_counts()

# Align labels
actual_counts = actual_counts.reindex(predicted_counts.index,
fill_value=0)
labels = LabelEncoder().fit_transform(predicted_counts.index)
```

```
# Plot comparison
width = 0.35
x = np.arange(len(labels))

plt.figure(figsize=(10, 6))
plt.bar(x - width/2, actual_counts, width, label='Actual',
color='lightblue')
plt.bar(x + width/2, predicted_counts, width, label='Predicted',
color='salmon')
plt.xticks(x, labels, rotation=45)
plt.title("Comparison of Actual vs. Predicted Log Counts")
plt.xlabel("Log Categories")
plt.ylabel("Count")
plt.legend()
plt.grid(axis='y')
plt.show()
```

Insights Gained from Visualization
1. **Prevalence of Issues**:
   o Distribution charts can highlight which issues occur most frequently, allowing IT teams to focus their efforts.
2. **Model Accuracy**:
   o Confusion matrices and performance metrics help evaluate the model's reliability in classifying logs.
3. **Key Influencing Factors**:
   o Feature importance charts show which log attributes (e.g. error messages or services) significantly impact predictions.
4. **Alignment of Predictions**:
   o Comparing actual vs. predicted counts reveals discrepancies, helping to identify areas where the model might need improvement.

4.9 Conclusion and Real-World Applications

Root Cause Analysis (RCA) is the backbone of effective IT operations management, enabling teams to swiftly identify, understand, and address system issues. By automating log classification with Machine Learning algorithms such as Random Forest and Logistic Regression, IT teams can significantly enhance their ability to manage incidents and ensure system reliability.

Throughout this chapter, we explored how data from system logs can be harnessed to pinpoint the root cause of failures. From understanding the structure of logs to preprocessing data and implementing robust classification algorithms, each step builds toward a comprehensive and efficient RCA process. Visualization of results further enhances interpretability, enabling stakeholders to gain actionable insights at a glance.

While Machine Learning models can greatly enhance RCA, their effectiveness depends on high-quality data, domain knowledge, and continuous refinement. With the right tools and practices, automated RCA is no longer a futuristic ideal but a present-day necessity for organizations seeking to maintain operational excellence.

Real-World Applications of Automated Log Classification
The automation of RCA and log classification has far-reaching implications across industries. Here, we delve into some practical applications and the benefits they bring to real-world IT operations.

1. Proactive Incident Management
- **Scenario**: A global e-commerce platform relies on real-time systems to process millions of transactions daily. Even minor system downtime can lead to substantial revenue losses.
- **Application**: Automated log classification detects early signs of database timeouts or network failures, allowing IT teams to intervene before customer-facing services are affected.
- **Benefit**: Reduces unplanned outages, improves system uptime, and enhances customer satisfaction.

2. Improved Security Monitoring
- **Scenario**: A financial institution faces constant threats from cyberattacks, such as unauthorized access attempts or DDoS attacks.
- **Application**: Logs containing patterns of failed login attempts or abnormal traffic spikes are automatically classified, flagging potential security breaches.
- **Benefit**: Enhances the organization's ability to respond to security incidents swiftly, protecting sensitive data and maintaining regulatory compliance.

3. Enhanced Scalability for Cloud Environments

- **Scenario**: A cloud service provider manages infrastructure for thousands of clients, generating extensive logs from distributed servers.
- **Application**: Automated RCA categorizes and prioritizes issues such as resource contention or VM failures, enabling faster resource allocation and scaling decisions.
- **Benefit**: Optimizes resource utilization, reduces operational costs, and ensures seamless client experiences.

4. Root Cause Analysis in IoT Networks

- **Scenario**: A smart city's IoT network includes sensors for traffic management, energy distribution, and environmental monitoring. Failures in these sensors can disrupt critical services.
- **Application**: Logs from IoT devices are analyzed to identify recurring issues like connectivity loss or hardware malfunctions.
- **Benefit**: Improves system reliability and ensures continuous service delivery for residents and city administrators.

5. Automation in DevOps Pipelines

- **Scenario**: A software development company employs CI/CD pipelines to deliver updates and patches regularly. Build failures or deployment errors can delay releases.
- **Application**: Logs from build processes are classified to identify whether failures stem from code errors, configuration issues, or environment incompatibilities.
- **Benefit**: Accelerates troubleshooting during development cycles, enabling faster time-to-market for new features.

The Road Ahead

As organizations continue to embrace digital transformation, the importance of efficient IT operations management grows exponentially. Log classification and automated RCA are just the beginning. The integration of Machine Learning with advanced technologies like AI-driven predictive analytics and real-time monitoring will further revolutionize how businesses operate.

For learners and professionals, this chapter serves as a foundation for understanding how data-driven RCA works and its immense potential. By mastering these techniques and tools, you position yourself to contribute to building smarter, more resilient systems in an increasingly complex digital landscape.

Automated RCA is not just a tool for troubleshooting—it's a strategic asset that ensures business continuity, enhances user experiences, and drives innovation. Let this knowledge empower you to embrace the future of IT operations management with confidence and creativity.

* * *

Incident Categorization
Using NLP

CHAPTER 5

INCIDENT CATEGORIZATION USING NLP

Incident categorization is a critical process in IT Service Management (ITSM), ensuring that reported issues are accurately classified and routed to the appropriate teams for resolution. This chapter focuses on leveraging NLP to automate IT incident categorization. By analyzing textual descriptions and matching them to predefined categories, the solution aims to:

- Minimize manual intervention.
- Optimize ticket routing processes.
- Contribute to the broader goal of efficient IT service delivery.

5.1 Introduction to Incident Categorization

This section explores the significance of categorization, the challenges associated with traditional methods, and the advantages of using automation powered by Natural Language Processing (NLP).

What is IT Incident Categorization?

IT incident categorization is the process of assigning predefined labels or categories to IT service tickets based on their descriptions. These categories often align with specific types of problems or the expertise required to resolve them. For example:

- **Categories:** Network Issues, Software Bugs, Hardware Failures, Security Breaches, etc.
- **Purpose:** Categorization helps in prioritizing, assigning, and resolving incidents systematically.

Why is Incident Categorization Important?

Proper incident categorization serves several purposes:

1. **Efficient Resource Allocation:** Ensures tickets are routed to the right teams with the expertise to address specific issues.
2. **Improved Resolution Time:** Reduces delays caused by misrouted tickets, enabling quicker responses and solutions.

3. **Enhanced Reporting and Analysis:** Categorized data helps in identifying recurring issues, bottlenecks, and areas for improvement in IT processes.
4. **Compliance and SLA Management:** Helps organizations meet Service Level Agreements (SLAs) by categorizing and prioritizing incidents appropriately.

Challenges in Manual Categorization
Despite its importance, manual categorization poses significant challenges:
1. **Human Error:** Misinterpretation of ticket descriptions often leads to incorrect categorization.
2. **Time-Consuming:** IT staff spend a considerable amount of time reviewing and categorizing tickets, especially in large organizations.
3. **Inconsistency:** Different individuals may categorize similar incidents differently, leading to confusion and inefficiency.
4. **Scalability Issues:** As the volume of incidents increases, manual methods become impractical.

The Role of Automation in Incident Categorization
Automating incident categorization with NLP addresses these challenges by:
1. **Improving Accuracy:** NLP models can understand textual data and categorize incidents with high precision.
2. **Reducing Time:** Automation processes tickets faster than manual methods, ensuring incidents are quickly routed to the right teams.
3. **Enhancing Consistency:** Machine-driven categorization ensures uniformity across all tickets.
4. **Scalability:** Automated systems can handle large volumes of tickets without compromising performance.

Key Benefits of NLP in Incident Categorization
- **Semantic Understanding:** NLP models like BERT can capture the meaning of complex ticket descriptions, even when users use varied terminology.
- **Dynamic Learning:** Machine Learning-based categorization systems can improve over time by learning from historical data and feedback.
- **Integration Capabilities:** NLP-driven categorization can be integrated seamlessly into existing ITSM tools, enhancing operational workflows.

5.2 Data Overview and Preprocessing
Automating IT incident categorization relies heavily on the quality and preparation of the input data. This section delves into the nature of the data used, common

challenges encountered in handling such data, and the steps taken to prepare it for building a robust NLP-based categorization model.

Input Data Description

The data used for this project consists of IT service tickets. These tickets typically include structured fields and unstructured textual descriptions, which are the primary focus for NLP-based analysis. Key attributes of the dataset are as follows:

1. **Incident ID:** A unique identifier for each service ticket.
2. **Description:** A detailed textual explanation of the issue reported. This field serves as the primary input for the NLP model.
   - Example: "Unable to connect to the company Wi-Fi on the 3rd floor."
3. **Category:** The target variable representing the category to which the incident belongs.
   - Example Categories: Network Issues, Software Bugs, Hardware Failures, Security Incidents, etc.
4. **Priority Level (Optional):** Indicates the urgency of resolving the ticket, which might influence routing but is not directly used in categorization.
5. **Other Metadata (Optional):** Fields like timestamp, location, or user role, which might provide additional context for downstream processes.

Dataset Overview

Fields

1. **Incident ID:** Unique identifier for each ticket (e.g. IT-10001, IT-10002).
2. **Description:** Textual explanation of the issue.
3. **Category:** The target label for classification (e.g. Network Issues, Software Bugs).
4. **Priority:** Urgency level (Low, Medium, High, Critical).
5. **Timestamp:** Date and time the ticket was reported.
6. **Location:** Optional field indicating the geographic or organizational location (e.g. HQ, Branch Office).
7. **Reporter Role:** Role of the user reporting the issue (e.g. Employee, IT Staff, Manager).

Categories

- Network Issues
- Software Bugs
- Hardware Failures
- Login/Authentication Issues
- Performance Degradation

- Security Incidents
- Data Access Issues

Dataset download link:

https://github.com/swapnilsaurav/ITOpExcellence/blob/main/IT_Incident_Datas
et.csv

Common Data Challenges
Working with IT service ticket data introduces several challenges:
1. **Textual Variability:**
    - Users describe incidents in varied ways, using different terminologies, abbreviations, and formats.
    - Example: "Wi-Fi not working" vs. "Unable to connect to wireless network."
2. **Imbalanced Categories:**
    - Certain categories, such as "Network Issues," might dominate the dataset, while others are underrepresented, leading to potential bias in the model.
3. **Noisy Data:**
    - Ticket descriptions may include irrelevant information, typos, or incomplete sentences, complicating text analysis.
4. **Duplicate Entries:**
    - Multiple tickets reporting the same issue may lead to redundancy in the dataset.
5. **Evolving Categories:**
    - New categories may emerge over time, requiring periodic model updates and retraining.

Data Preprocessing Steps
To address these challenges and prepare the data for modeling, the following preprocessing steps are implemented:
1. **Data Cleaning:**
    - Remove special characters, HTML tags, and unnecessary symbols from ticket descriptions.
    - Standardize text by converting it to lowercase.
    - Correct common spelling errors using text normalization techniques.

2. **Tokenization:**
   - Split textual descriptions into individual tokens (words or subwords) for further processing.
   - Example: "Unable to connect to Wi-Fi" → ["unable," "to," "connect," "to," "wi-fi"].

3. **Stop Word Removal:**
   - Eliminate frequently occurring but non-informative words such as "the," "is," and "and."
   - Ensures the focus remains on meaningful terms in the ticket description.

4. **Lemmatization:**
   - Reduce words to their base or root form to standardize the vocabulary.
   - Example: "connecting," "connected," "connects" → "connect."

5. **Handling Imbalanced Data:**
   - Employ techniques like oversampling (duplicating minority class samples), undersampling (reducing majority class samples), or using class weights during model training.

6. **Text Vectorization:**
   - Convert textual data into numerical representations suitable for Machine Learning models:
     - **TF-IDF (Term Frequency-Inverse Document Frequency):** Represents the importance of words relative to the entire dataset.
     - **Word Embeddings (e.g. BERT):** Generate semantic representations of words and phrases to capture contextual meaning.

7. **Duplicate Detection and Removal:**
   - Identify and eliminate duplicate entries to ensure data quality and prevent model overfitting to repeated patterns.

8. **Splitting Data:**
   - Divide the dataset into training, validation, and test sets to enable robust model evaluation and reduce overfitting.

Python Implementation:

```python
import pandas as pd
import re
from sklearn.feature_extraction.text import TfidfVectorizer
```

```
# Load the dataset
file_path = "IT_Incident_Dataset.csv"
df = pd.read_csv(file_path)

# Step 1: Data Cleaning
def clean_text(text):
    text = re.sub(r'[^\w\s]', '', text)  # Remove special
characters and punctuation
    text = re.sub(r'\s+', ' ', text)  # Replace multiple spaces
with a single space
    text = text.lower()  # Convert text to lowercase
    return text.strip()

df['Cleaned_Description'] = df['Description'].apply(clean_text)

# Step 2: Tokenization
df['Tokenized_Description'] =
df['Cleaned_Description'].apply(lambda x: x.split())

# Step 3: Stop Word Removal
stop_words = set(["the", "is", "in", "to", "and", "a", "on", "of",
"for", "by", "with"])
df['Tokenized_Description'] = df['Tokenized_Description'].apply(
    lambda x: [word for word in x if word not in stop_words]
)

# Step 4: Simple Lemmatization (for demonstration purposes)
df['Tokenized_Description'] = df['Tokenized_Description'].apply(
    lambda x: [word.rstrip('s') for word in x]  # Remove simple
plural endings
)

# Step 5: Vectorization using TF-IDF
tfidf_vectorizer = TfidfVectorizer(max_features=500)
tfidf_matrix =
tfidf_vectorizer.fit_transform(df['Cleaned_Description'])

# Add TF-IDF features to the DataFrame
tfidf_features = pd.DataFrame(
    tfidf_matrix.toarray(),
    columns=tfidf_vectorizer.get_feature_names_out()
)

df_with_tfidf = pd.concat([df.reset_index(drop=True),
tfidf_features.reset_index(drop=True)], axis=1)

# Save the preprocessed dataset
```

```
processed_file_path = "Preprocessed_IT_Incident_Dataset.csv"
df_with_tfidf.to_csv(processed_file_path, index=False)

print(f"Preprocessed dataset saved to {processed_file_path}")
```

Here's a concise summary of the preprocessing steps:
1. **Data Cleaning**: Remove special characters, punctuation, and extra spaces, and convert text to lowercase to ensure uniformity.
2. **Tokenization**: Split the cleaned text into individual words (tokens).
3. **Stop Word Removal**: Eliminate commonly used but non-informative words like "the," "is," and "to" from the tokenized text.
4. **Lemmatization**: Simplify words to their base or root form by removing basic plural endings (e.g. "systems" → "system").
5. **Vectorization**: Use TF-IDF (Term Frequency-Inverse Document Frequency) to convert textual data into numerical features, capturing the importance of words across the dataset.
6. **Integration**: Combine the original data and TF-IDF features into a single dataset for further analysis or model building.

Exploratory Data Analysis (EDA)
Before proceeding to model training, exploratory analysis is conducted to gain insights into the dataset:
1. **Category Distribution:**
   o Visualize the frequency of each category to identify imbalances.
   o Example: Plot a bar chart showing the number of tickets per category.
2. **Text Length Analysis:**
   o Examine the average number of words in ticket descriptions to ensure consistent input length.
3. **Keyword Analysis:**
   o Identify common terms associated with each category to verify alignment with domain knowledge.
4. **Outlier Detection:**
   o Spot and handle anomalies in ticket descriptions or other metadata fields.

Tools and Libraries Used
- **Data Cleaning and Preprocessing:**
   o Libraries: NLTK, SpaCy, pandas, NumPy

- **Text Vectorization:**
  - o Tools: Scikit-learn (TF-IDF), Hugging Face Transformers (BERT)
- **EDA and Visualization:**
  - o Tools: Matplotlib, Seaborn, Plotly

Python code for Exploratory Data Analysis

```python
import pandas as pd
import matplotlib.pyplot as plt
import seaborn as sns

# Load the preprocessed dataset
file_path = "Preprocessed_IT_Incident_Dataset.csv"
df = pd.read_csv(file_path)

# Step 1: Overview of the Data
print("Data Overview:")
print(df.info())
print("\nSummary Statistics:")
print(df.describe())

# Step 2: Check Missing Values
missing_values = df.isnull().sum()
print("\nMissing Values:")
print(missing_values)

# Step 3: Distribution of Incident Categories
plt.figure(figsize=(10, 6))
df['Category'].value_counts().plot(kind='bar', color='skyblue')
plt.title('Distribution of Incident Categories')
plt.xlabel('Category')
plt.ylabel('Count')
plt.xticks(rotation=45)
plt.tight_layout()
plt.show()

# Step 4: Distribution of Priorities
plt.figure(figsize=(8, 5))
df['Priority'].value_counts().plot(kind='bar', color='salmon')
plt.title('Distribution of Incident Priorities')
plt.xlabel('Priority')
plt.ylabel('Count')
plt.xticks(rotation=0)
plt.tight_layout()
plt.show()
```

```
# Step 5: Word Frequency Analysis
def plot_word_frequencies(column, top_n=20):
    from collections import Counter
    word_list = df[column].dropna().apply(eval).sum()  # Convert
string representation of list to actual list
    word_counts = Counter(word_list).most_common(top_n)
    words, counts = zip(*word_counts)
    plt.figure(figsize=(10, 6))
    sns.barplot(x=list(counts), y=list(words), palette='viridis')
    plt.title(f'Top {top_n} Most Common Words in {column}')
    plt.xlabel('Frequency')
    plt.ylabel('Words')
    plt.tight_layout()
    plt.show()

plot_word_frequencies('Tokenized_Description')
```

Importance of Preprocessing

Effective preprocessing lays the foundation for building a successful NLP model. By addressing data quality issues and transforming textual descriptions into meaningful representations, this step ensures:

- Improved model performance.
- Enhanced interpretability of results.
- Reduced risks of overfitting or underfitting.

5.3 Algorithm Selection and Design

Effective IT incident categorization requires models capable of understanding and analyzing textual data. Two primary approaches are discussed:

1. **BERT (Bidirectional Encoder Representations from Transformers):**
   - **Overview:**
     - BERT is a state-of-the-art transformer-based NLP model developed by Google.
     - It uses bidirectional training of transformers to capture the context of words based on their position in a sentence.
   - **Application in Text Classification:**
     - BERT embeddings can encode the semantic meaning of ticket descriptions, allowing the model to understand context-sensitive phrases.
     - Fine-tuning BERT for incident categorization aligns its pre-trained knowledge with the specific domain of IT incidents.

2. **TF-IDF (Term Frequency-Inverse Document Frequency) with Naive Bayes:**
    o **Overview:**
        ▪ TF-IDF is a statistical technique that converts textual data into numerical representations based on the frequency and uniqueness of words.
        ▪ Naive Bayes is a probabilistic classifier that assumes conditional independence between features.
    o **Application in Text Classification:**
        ▪ TF-IDF provides a simple, interpretable representation of textual data.
        ▪ When paired with Naive Bayes, it offers a lightweight solution for quick and reliable categorization, especially for smaller datasets.

Feature Engineering

Feature engineering transforms raw textual data into meaningful representations that can be used by Machine Learning models.

1. **Creating Word Embeddings with TF-IDF:**
    o Words in ticket descriptions are vectorized using TF-IDF, which captures:
        ▪ **Term Frequency (TF):** How often a word appears in a document.
        ▪ **Inverse Document Frequency (IDF):** How unique a word is across all documents.
    o This approach emphasizes domain-specific terms while reducing the impact of common, less-informative words.
2. **Using Pre-trained BERT Embeddings:**
    o BERT generates dense vector representations of ticket descriptions by encoding the semantic relationships between words.
    o Pre-trained embeddings provide a strong starting point, leveraging vast knowledge from training on general corpora like Wikipedia and BooksCorpus.
    o Fine-tuning adapts these embeddings to the IT domain, improving accuracy for categorization tasks.

Model Architecture

The model architecture is designed to combine preprocessing, feature extraction, and classification into an efficient pipeline. Below is the high-level design:

1. **Input Layer:**
   - Accepts raw textual descriptions from IT tickets.
2. **Preprocessing Module:**
   - Cleans and tokenizes the text.
   - Applies stop-word removal and lemmatization.
   - Optionally augments text with domain-specific synonyms or context.
3. **Feature Extraction Module:**
   - **TF-IDF Vectorization:** Converts text into sparse numerical vectors for simpler models.
   - **BERT Embeddings:** Generates dense semantic vectors for deeper models.
4. **Classification Module:**
   - **Naive Bayes Classifier (with TF-IDF):**
     - Lightweight and interpretable model.
     - Suitable for scenarios with limited computational resources.
   - **Fine-Tuned BERT Classifier:**
     - State-of-the-art performance for complex, context-sensitive descriptions.
     - Suitable for large datasets or high-accuracy requirements.
5. **Output Layer:**
   - Predicts the incident category.
   - Optionally provides a confidence score for the prediction.
6. **Error Handling:**
   - Low-confidence predictions are flagged for manual review.
   - Logs are generated to capture errors for iterative improvements.

5.4 Implementing TF-IDF Using Python

Automate the categorization of IT incident tickets based on textual descriptions to reduce manual effort, minimize resolution time, and ensure accurate routing to the appropriate teams.

The Python code has been updated to include a complete implementation for automating IT incident categorization using TF-IDF and Naive Bayes. It handles data cleaning, vectorization, model training, evaluation, and saving the trained model and vectorizer for future use.

```python
import pandas as pd
from sklearn.model_selection import train_test_split
from sklearn.feature_extraction.text import TfidfVectorizer
from sklearn.naive_bayes import MultinomialNB
from sklearn.metrics import classification_report, accuracy_score,
confusion_matrix
import seaborn as sns
import matplotlib.pyplot as plt

# Load the dataset
file_path = "IT_Incident_Dataset.csv"
df = pd.read_csv(file_path)

# Data Cleaning Function
def clean_text(text):
    import re
    text = re.sub(r'[^\w\s]', '', text)   # Remove special
characters and punctuation
    text = re.sub(r'\s+', ' ', text)   # Replace multiple spaces
with a single space
    text = text.lower()   # Convert text to lowercase
    return text.strip()

# Clean the descriptions
df['Cleaned_Description'] = df['Description'].apply(clean_text)

# Prepare features and target
X = df['Cleaned_Description']
y = df['Category']

# Split the dataset into training and testing sets
X_train, X_test, y_train, y_test = train_test_split(X, y,
test_size=0.2, random_state=42, stratify=y)

# TF-IDF Vectorization
tfidf_vectorizer = TfidfVectorizer(max_features=500)
X_train_tfidf = tfidf_vectorizer.fit_transform(X_train)
X_test_tfidf = tfidf_vectorizer.transform(X_test)

# Train a Naive Bayes Classifier
naive_bayes_model = MultinomialNB()
naive_bayes_model.fit(X_train_tfidf, y_train)

# Make Predictions
```

```python
y_pred = naive_bayes_model.predict(X_test_tfidf)

# Evaluate the Model
accuracy = accuracy_score(y_test, y_pred)
print(f"Accuracy: {accuracy:.2f}")
print("\nClassification Report:\n")
print(classification_report(y_test, y_pred))

# Confusion Matrix
conf_matrix = confusion_matrix(y_test, y_pred)
plt.figure(figsize=(10, 8))
sns.heatmap(conf_matrix, annot=True, fmt='d', cmap='Blues',
xticklabels=naive_bayes_model.classes_,
yticklabels=naive_bayes_model.classes_)
plt.title('Confusion Matrix')
plt.xlabel('Predicted Labels')
plt.ylabel('True Labels')
plt.show()

# Save the vectorizer and model for future use
import pickle
with open("tfidf_vectorizer.pkl", "wb") as tfidf_file:
    pickle.dump(tfidf_vectorizer, tfidf_file)

with open("naive_bayes_model.pkl", "wb") as model_file:
    pickle.dump(naive_bayes_model, model_file)

print("Model and vectorizer saved.")

# Test the model with new examples
def test_model(new_descriptions):
    cleaned_descriptions = [clean_text(desc) for desc in
new_descriptions]
    vectorized_descriptions =
tfidf_vectorizer.transform(cleaned_descriptions)
    predictions =
naive_bayes_model.predict(vectorized_descriptions)
    for desc, pred in zip(new_descriptions, predictions):
        print(f"Description: {desc}\nPredicted Category: {pred}\n")

# Example test cases
test_descriptions = [
    "Unable to connect to the company Wi-Fi.",
    "The application crashes whenever I click submit.",
    "Detected unauthorized login attempt on the server.",
    "Printer is showing a paper jam error."
]
```

```
test_model(test_descriptions)
```

Output:
```
Description: Unable to connect to the company Wi-Fi.
Predicted Category: Network Issues

Description: The application crashes whenever I click submit.
Predicted Category: Software Bugs

Description: Detected unauthorized login attempt on the server.
Predicted Category: Security Incidents

Description: Printer is showing a paper jam error.
Predicted Category: Hardware Failures
```

Explanation of the code:
1. Data Loading
df = pd.read_csv(file_path)
- **Purpose**: Load the dataset from a CSV file.
- **df**: The dataframe that holds all the data.

2. Data Cleaning
- Removes special characters, punctuation, and extra spaces.
- Converts all text to lowercase to ensure uniformity.

df['Cleaned_Description'] = df['Description'].apply(clean_text)
- Applies the cleaning function to the Description column and creates a new column Cleaned_Description.

3. Feature Preparation
- **X**: Features (cleaned descriptions).
- **y**: Target labels (categories of incidents).

4. Data Splitting
- Splits the dataset into training (80%) and testing (20%) sets.
- Ensures the category distribution in y is maintained across splits using stratify=y.

5. Text Vectorization

tfidf_vectorizer = TfidfVectorizer(max_features=500)

X_train_tfidf = tfidf_vectorizer.fit_transform(X_train)

X_test_tfidf = tfidf_vectorizer.transform(X_test)

- **TF-IDF** converts textual descriptions into numerical features by considering the importance of words.
- **max_features=500**: Limits the vectorizer to the 500 most important words.
- **fit_transform**: Fits the vectorizer to the training data and transforms it into a numerical matrix.
- **transform**: Transforms the test data using the same vectorizer.

6. Model Training

- Trains a **Multinomial Naive Bayes** classifier on the TF-IDF vectors of the training data.

7. Model Evaluation

- **predict**: Makes predictions on the test set.
- **Accuracy**: The percentage of correctly classified incidents.
- **Classification Report**: Provides precision, recall, and F1-score for each category.

8. Confusion Matrix

- Visualizes how well the model classified each category.
- **True Labels**: The actual category.
- **Predicted Labels**: The category predicted by the model.

9. Model and Vectorizer Saving

- Saves the trained vectorizer and model for future use without retraining.

10. Testing the Model

- **Purpose**: Allows you to test the model on new incident descriptions.
- **Workflow**:
    1. Cleans the input descriptions.
    2. Vectorizes them using the saved TF-IDF vectorizer.
    3. Predicts the category using the trained Naive Bayes model.
    4. Displays the description and predicted category.

11. Example Testing
- Provides example descriptions to test the model and outputs the predicted categories.

5.5 Implementing BERT Using Python

Objective: Leverage state-of-the-art natural language processing using BERT to automate IT incident categorization with high accuracy. This approach aims to minimize human intervention, reduce resolution time, and ensure precise routing to the appropriate teams.

Below is the implementation for using a BERT-based classifier on the IT incident dataset. The code includes preprocessing, model definition, training, evaluation, and prediction.

```python
import pandas as pd
import torch
from transformers import BertTokenizer,
BertForSequenceClassification
from torch.utils.data import DataLoader, Dataset
from sklearn.model_selection import train_test_split
from sklearn.metrics import classification_report
from torch.optim import Adam
from tqdm import tqdm

# Load the dataset
file_path = "IT_Incident_Dataset.csv"
df = pd.read_csv(file_path)

# Data Cleaning Function
def clean_text(text):
    import re
    text = re.sub(r'[^\w\s]', '', text)  # Remove special
characters and punctuation
    text = re.sub(r'\s+', ' ', text)  # Replace multiple spaces
with a single space
    text = text.lower()  # Convert text to lowercase
    return text.strip()

# Clean the descriptions
df['Cleaned_Description'] = df['Description'].apply(clean_text)

# Prepare features and target
X = df['Cleaned_Description'].tolist()
y = df['Category'].tolist()
```

```python
# Split the dataset into training and testing sets
X_train, X_test, y_train, y_test = train_test_split(X, y,
test_size=0.2, random_state=42, stratify=y)

# Label Encoding
from sklearn.preprocessing import LabelEncoder
label_encoder = LabelEncoder()
y_train_encoded = label_encoder.fit_transform(y_train)
y_test_encoded = label_encoder.transform(y_test)

# Define a custom dataset class
class IncidentDataset(Dataset):
    def __init__(self, texts, labels, tokenizer, max_length):
        self.texts = texts
        self.labels = labels
        self.tokenizer = tokenizer
        self.max_length = max_length

    def __len__(self):
        return len(self.texts)

    def __getitem__(self, idx):
        text = self.texts[idx]
        label = self.labels[idx]
        encoding = self.tokenizer(
            text,
            max_length=self.max_length,
            padding='max_length',
            truncation=True,
            return_tensors="pt"
        )
        return {
            'input_ids': encoding['input_ids'].squeeze(0),
            'attention_mask':
encoding['attention_mask'].squeeze(0),
            'label': torch.tensor(label, dtype=torch.long)
        }

# Tokenizer and Dataset Preparation
tokenizer = BertTokenizer.from_pretrained('bert-base-uncased')
max_length = 128
train_dataset = IncidentDataset(X_train, y_train_encoded,
tokenizer, max_length)
test_dataset = IncidentDataset(X_test, y_test_encoded, tokenizer,
max_length)

# DataLoader
```

```python
train_loader = DataLoader(train_dataset, batch_size=16,
shuffle=True)
test_loader = DataLoader(test_dataset, batch_size=16)

# Model Definition
model = BertForSequenceClassification.from_pretrained('bert-base-
uncased', num_labels=len(label_encoder.classes_))

# Optimizer and Loss Function
optimizer = Adam(model.parameters(), lr=2e-5)
criterion = torch.nn.CrossEntropyLoss()

device = torch.device('cuda' if torch.cuda.is_available() else
'cpu')
model.to(device)

# Training Loop
epochs = 3
model.train()
for epoch in range(epochs):
    loop = tqdm(train_loader, leave=True)
    for batch in loop:
        input_ids = batch['input_ids'].to(device)
        attention_mask = batch['attention_mask'].to(device)
        labels = batch['label'].to(device)

        optimizer.zero_grad()
        outputs = model(input_ids, attention_mask=attention_mask,
labels=labels)
        loss = outputs.loss
        loss.backward()
        optimizer.step()

        loop.set_description(f'Epoch {epoch}')
        loop.set_postfix(loss=loss.item())

# Evaluation
model.eval()
predictions, true_labels = [], []
with torch.no_grad():
    for batch in test_loader:
        input_ids = batch['input_ids'].to(device)
        attention_mask = batch['attention_mask'].to(device)
        labels = batch['label'].to(device)
        outputs = model(input_ids, attention_mask=attention_mask)
        logits = outputs.logits
        preds = torch.argmax(logits, axis=1)
        predictions.extend(preds.cpu().numpy())
```

```python
        true_labels.extend(labels.cpu().numpy())

# Classification Report
print("\nClassification Report:\n")
print(classification_report(true_labels, predictions,
target_names=label_encoder.classes_))

# Save the model
model.save_pretrained("bert_incident_model")
tokenizer.save_pretrained("bert_incident_model")

print("Model and tokenizer saved.")

# Test with new descriptions
def test_bert_model(descriptions):
    model.eval()
    encoded_descriptions = tokenizer(
        descriptions,
        max_length=max_length,
        padding='max_length',
        truncation=True,
        return_tensors="pt"
    )
    input_ids = encoded_descriptions['input_ids'].to(device)
    attention_mask =
encoded_descriptions['attention_mask'].to(device)
    with torch.no_grad():
        outputs = model(input_ids, attention_mask=attention_mask)
        logits = outputs.logits
        predictions = torch.argmax(logits, axis=1).cpu().numpy()
    decoded_predictions =
label_encoder.inverse_transform(predictions)
    for desc, pred in zip(descriptions, decoded_predictions):
        print(f"Description: {desc}\nPredicted Category: {pred}\n")

# Example test cases
test_descriptions = [
    "Unable to connect to the company Wi-Fi.",
    "The application crashes whenever I click submit.",
    "Detected unauthorized login attempt on the server.",
    "Printer is showing a paper jam error."
]

test_bert_model(test_descriptions)
```

Here's a detailed explanation of the above code:

1. Data Loading and Cleaning
- Loads the dataset from the file.
- Cleans text by removing unwanted characters, normalizing spaces, and converting text to lowercase.

2. Data Preparation
- **X**: The textual descriptions after cleaning.
- **y**: The corresponding categories.
- Splits the data into training (80%) and testing (20%) sets.
- Encodes the categorical labels into integers for compatibility with the BERT model.

3. Custom Dataset for BERT
- Prepares the data for BERT by tokenizing text and creating PyTorch tensors for input IDs, attention masks, and labels.

4. Tokenization and DataLoader
- Uses the **BERT tokenizer** to tokenize the input text.
- Creates **DataLoader** objects for training and testing.

5. Model Definition
- Initializes the BERT model with a classification head to predict categories. The number of output labels equals the number of unique categories.

6. Training Loop
- Trains the model for a specified number of epochs:
  - Moves data to the **device** (CPU/GPU).
  - Computes the loss.
  - Performs backpropagation and updates model weights.

7. Evaluation
- Evaluates the model on the test set without computing gradients.

8. Classification Report
- Generates metrics like precision, recall, and F1-score for each category.

9. Model and Tokenizer Saving
- Saves the trained model and tokenizer for future use.

10. Testing with New Descriptions
- Allows for testing the model with new, unseen text descriptions.
- Outputs the predicted categories.

11. Example Testing
- Uses a set of example descriptions to test the model's prediction capability.

5.6 Algorithm Selection

Algorithm selection is a critical step in designing a solution for automating IT incident categorization. It requires balancing the complexity, interpretability, accuracy, and computational cost of various Machine Learning and natural language processing (NLP) approaches. In this section, we outline the decision-making process for selecting the most appropriate algorithms for the task and explore their strengths and limitations.

Classical Machine Learning Approaches
TF-IDF + Naive Bayes
- **Strengths**:
    - Simple and computationally efficient.
    - Works well on small to medium-sized datasets.
    - Provides interpretable results, with the ability to analyze word importance.
- **Limitations**:
    - Lacks context-awareness; cannot effectively capture relationships between words or their sequence.
    - Limited scalability for highly complex or large datasets.

Support Vector Machines (SVM)
- **Strengths**:
    - Effective for high-dimensional text data.
    - Robust to overfitting, especially in small datasets.
- **Limitations**:
    - Computationally expensive for large datasets.
    - Requires careful tuning of hyperparameters.

Deep Learning-Based NLP Models
Recurrent Neural Networks (RNNs) and LSTMs
- **Strengths**:
    - Captures sequential dependencies in text, making it suitable for longer descriptions.

o   Handles context better than traditional methods.
- **Limitations**:
    o   Computationally intensive and slower to train.
    o   Struggles with very long texts or complex dependencies.

Transformer-Based Models (BERT)
- **Strengths**:
    o   State-of-the-art performance in text classification tasks.
    o   Captures bidirectional context, understanding words based on their surrounding words.
    o   Pre-trained on large corpora, requiring minimal additional data for fine-tuning.
- **Limitations**:
    o   Requires significant computational resources.
    o   Less interpretable than simpler models like Naive Bayes.

Considerations for Future Enhancements
1. **Multilingual Support**:
    o   Use models like XLM-RoBERTa to handle tickets in multiple languages.
2. **Domain-Specific Fine-Tuning**:
    o   Fine-tune BERT with IT-specific corpora for better performance on domain-specific language.
3. **Active Learning**:
    o   Employ active learning to iteratively improve model performance by incorporating feedback from human experts.

Algorithm selection reflects the trade-offs between simplicity and sophistication, aligning with the business goals of reducing resolution time and ensuring efficient ticket routing. This robust selection process sets the foundation for effective IT service management solutions.

Conclusion

Natural Language Processing (NLP) has emerged as a transformative force in IT operations, offering unprecedented capabilities to analyze and automate complex processes. This chapter focused on leveraging NLP for IT incident categorization—a critical task in IT Service Management (ITSM)—to improve efficiency, accuracy, and scalability.

NLP plays a pivotal role in transforming IT operations by addressing challenges that arise from unstructured data, such as service ticket descriptions. Key benefits of NLP in IT operations include:

1. **Automating Repetitive Tasks**:
   o   NLP enables the automation of manual processes like categorizing, prioritizing, and routing tickets, freeing up IT personnel for more strategic tasks.
2. **Enhancing Decision-Making**:
   o   By extracting insights from unstructured text, NLP provides actionable data to improve IT processes, optimize resource allocation, and enhance service quality.
3. **Scalability**:
   o   NLP models, especially transformer-based architectures like BERT, can process large volumes of text data efficiently, making them suitable for organizations of all sizes.
4. **Reducing Human Error**:
   o   By standardizing and automating tasks, NLP minimizes errors that often occur in manual categorization, ensuring consistent and reliable results.
5. **Improving User Experience**:
   o   Faster and more accurate ticket resolution enhances customer satisfaction and fosters trust in IT services.

Broader Implications of NLP in ITSM

Beyond incident categorization, NLP has broader applications in IT operations:

- **Predictive Analytics**: Anticipating recurring issues based on historical ticket data.
- **Chatbots and Virtual Assistants**: Providing instant responses to user queries and resolving simpler issues autonomously.
- **Sentiment Analysis**: Gauging user satisfaction from feedback and interactions.
- **Anomaly Detection**: Identifying unusual patterns in IT logs and alerts.

By integrating these capabilities, NLP can drive a shift from reactive to proactive IT management, aligning operations with the goals of digital transformation.

NLP is revolutionizing IT operations, bridging the gap between unstructured data and actionable insights. By automating repetitive tasks, reducing response times, and enabling data-driven decision-making, NLP empowers IT teams to operate more efficiently and focus on strategic initiatives. As the technology continues to evolve, its integration into ITSM will pave the way for smarter, more adaptive, and user-centric IT operations, ultimately transforming the way organizations manage their technology ecosystems.

* * *

Security Threat Detection Using Behavioral Analytics

CHAPTER 6

SECURITY THREAT DETECTION USING BEHAVIORAL ANALYTICS

Security threat detection has become a cornerstone of modern cybersecurity strategies. With the proliferation of digital systems and the increasing sophistication of cyberattacks, organizations face significant challenges in safeguarding sensitive information and ensuring the integrity of their operations. This chapter explores how behavioral analytics can revolutionize threat detection by identifying unusual activity patterns indicative of potential security breaches.

In today's interconnected world, organizations are more vulnerable than ever to cybersecurity threats. Some key reasons why effective threat detection is crucial include:

- **Escalating Threat Landscape**:
    - o The number of cyberattacks has grown exponentially, ranging from phishing and ransomware to insider threats and advanced persistent threats (APTs).
- **Cost of Data Breaches**:
    - o According to industry reports, the average cost of a data breach runs into millions of dollars, not to mention the reputational damage to organizations.
- **Regulatory Compliance**:
    - o Strict data protection regulations (e.g. GDPR, HIPAA) mandate robust security measures to detect and mitigate potential threats.

Traditional security measures like signature-based detection systems often fail to detect novel or zero-day attacks, creating an urgent need for more adaptive and intelligent approaches.

Role of Behavioral Analytics in Security
Behavioral analytics focuses on monitoring and analyzing the behavior of users, systems, and networks to identify deviations from normal patterns. This approach is particularly effective in detecting:

- **Insider Threats**:
  - o Malicious actions by employees or contractors that bypass traditional security measures.
- **Compromised Accounts**:
  - o Unauthorized access resulting from stolen credentials.
- **Advanced Persistent Threats (APTs)**:
  - o Long-term, targeted attacks that operate under the radar of conventional systems.

Key Benefits of Behavioral Analytics:
1. **Proactive Detection**:
   - o Unlike signature-based methods, behavioral analytics identifies unknown threats by recognizing unusual patterns.
2. **Context-Aware Monitoring**:
   - o By understanding the context of user and system behavior, it can distinguish between legitimate and malicious actions.
3. **Scalability**:
   - o Behavioral models can adapt to evolving environments and handle vast amounts of log data in real time.

6.1. Data Collection and Understanding

The cornerstone of any robust security threat detection system lies in its data. Behavioral analytics thrives on rich, well-structured information about user activities, system interactions, and network patterns. This section explores the types of data used in security threat detection, the preprocessing steps required to make this data analysis-ready, and the insights gained through exploratory data analysis (EDA). The synthetic dataset generated for this chapter serves as an illustrative foundation, simulating real-world security logs for deeper understanding.

Types of Input Data
Security threat detection relies on collecting diverse types of data that capture user and system behaviors. These data types include user activities, system logs, and contextual information that help identify unusual patterns. The dataset used in this chapter incorporates several key elements:

1. **User Access Logs**
   Logs tracking user login and logout events are fundamental to understanding access patterns. Failed login attempts are particularly critical, as they often signal potential unauthorized access attempts.

2. **Session Data**
   - **Session Duration**: Calculated from login and logout timestamps, session durations help identify deviations in normal activity. For example, abnormally long sessions may indicate compromised accounts left open for malicious purposes.
   - **In-Session Actions**: Details of user activities during their session, such as accessing files or modifying configurations.

3. **System Interaction Data**
   - **Resource Access**: Logs interactions with critical resources such as servers, databases, and files. Repeated or unusual access to sensitive resources can indicate insider threats.
   - **Configuration Changes**: Captures modifications to system settings, which could indicate attempts to weaken security controls.

4. **Network Data**
   - **IP Addresses**: Tracks the origin of user activities, aiding in geolocation and detection of access from suspicious regions.
   - **Geographical Locations**: Categorizes actions based on physical or organizational locations, such as HQ, branch offices, or remote connections.

5. **Security Indicators**
   - **Success or Failure**: For actions like logins, this field indicates whether the attempt was successful, helping distinguish normal activities from potential threats.

Examples of Security-Relevant Features:
- IP addresses and geolocations reveal login attempts from unexpected regions.
- Resource access patterns help detect unusual interactions with critical systems.
- Session durations and failed login rates provide clues to suspicious activity.

Data Preprocessing

Preprocessing transforms raw security data into a clean, structured format suitable for analysis and modelling. This step ensures that the data is not only usable but also enriched with meaningful features to enhance detection accuracy.

1. **Data Cleaning**
   - Duplicate entries are removed to prevent overrepresentation in analysis.
   - Irrelevant logs or incomplete records, such as those lacking user IDs or timestamps, are filtered out.

2. **Normalization**
   - Standardizing formats for IP addresses, timestamps, and resource names ensures consistency across the dataset.
   - Time zones are normalized to allow accurate comparison of activities across regions.

3. **Handling Missing Values**
   - Missing location data can be inferred from IP addresses if available.
   - Session durations with missing logout timestamps can be approximated using the median duration for that user.

4. **Outlier Detection and Handling**
   - Abnormal values, such as excessively long or short session durations, are capped at reasonable thresholds to prevent skewing results.

5. **Feature Aggregation**
   Aggregating raw data into derived metrics provides actionable insights:
   - **Session Frequency**: Tracks the number of logins per user within a specific timeframe.
   - **Average Session Duration**: Measures the typical session length for each user.
   - **Failed Login Rate**: Calculates the proportion of failed login attempts to total attempts.
   - **Resource Access Frequency**: Identifies users with high interaction rates with sensitive systems.

Exploratory Data Analysis (EDA)

EDA bridges the gap between raw data and actionable insights, allowing security teams to visualize behaviors, uncover patterns, and detect anomalies.

1. **Visualization of Typical Behaviors**
   - o **Login Frequency**: Histograms or bar plots reveal the distribution of login frequencies across users, highlighting those with unusually high activity.
   - o **Session Duration**: Boxplots or line charts show the range and distribution of session durations, helping to identify abnormal values.
   - o **Action Distribution**: Pie charts or bar graphs display the proportions of different actions (e.g. Login, File Access, Configuration Change), providing an overview of typical user activities.

2. **Geographical Analysis**
   - o **Location-Based Activity**: Heatmaps visualize the intensity of actions across locations like HQ or remote offices, identifying regions with heightened activity.
   - o **IP-Based Anomalies**: Scatter plots of IP addresses detect logins from unrecognized or unusual regions.

3. **Anomaly Detection**
   - o **Failed Login Patterns**: Line plots reveal spikes in failed login attempts, potentially indicating brute force attacks.
   - o **Resource Access Outliers**: Boxplots highlight users who access sensitive resources at rates significantly higher than average.

4. **Correlation Analysis**
   - o Examining relationships between features, such as session duration and resource access frequency, helps identify patterns that may indicate normal behavior or potential threats.
   - o Correlation matrices visually represent these relationships, informing feature selection for modelling.

```python
import pandas as pd
import numpy as np
import matplotlib.pyplot as plt
import seaborn as sns

# Load the synthetic dataset
data_path = "Security_Threat_Dataset.csv"
df = pd.read_csv(data_path)
```

```python
# Display the first few rows of the dataset
print("Dataset Preview:")
print(df.head())

# Step 1: Data Cleaning
print("\nCleaning Data...")
# Remove duplicate entries
df.drop_duplicates(inplace=True)

# Filter rows with missing essential fields like UserID or
Timestamp
df = df.dropna(subset=['UserID', 'Timestamp'])

# Normalize IP addresses and Resource fields
print("Normalizing Data...")
df['IP_Address'] = df['IP_Address'].str.strip()
df['Resource'] = df['Resource'].str.strip().fillna('N/A')

# Convert Timestamp to datetime format
df['Timestamp'] = pd.to_datetime(df['Timestamp'])

# Step 2: Feature Aggregation
print("Aggregating Features...")
# Create a 'Session Duration' column (dummy value for now since no
logout timestamp exists)
df['Session_Duration'] = np.where(df['Action'] == 'Logout',
np.random.randint(5, 120, size=len(df)), np.nan)

# Calculate failed login rate per user
failed_login_rate = df[df['Action'] ==
'Failed_Login'].groupby('UserID').size() /
df.groupby('UserID').size()
failed_login_rate =
failed_login_rate.fillna(0).rename('Failed_Login_Rate')

# Count of actions by user
action_counts =
df.groupby('UserID')['Action'].count().rename('Action_Count')

# Combine aggregated metrics into a single DataFrame
aggregated_metrics = pd.concat([failed_login_rate, action_counts],
axis=1)
print("Aggregated Metrics Preview:")
print(aggregated_metrics.head())

# Step 3: Exploratory Data Analysis (EDA)
print("\nPerforming EDA...")
```

```python
# 3.1 Login Frequency Distribution
plt.figure(figsize=(10, 6))
login_counts = df[df['Action'] == 'Login']['UserID'].value_counts()
login_counts.hist(bins=20, color='skyblue', edgecolor='black')
plt.title("Login Frequency Distribution")
plt.xlabel("Number of Logins")
plt.ylabel("Frequency")
plt.grid(axis='y')
plt.show()

# 3.2 Session Duration Distribution
plt.figure(figsize=(10, 6))
plt.hist(df['Session_Duration'].dropna(), bins=20, color='salmon',
edgecolor='black')
plt.title("Session Duration Distribution")
plt.xlabel("Session Duration (minutes)")
plt.ylabel("Frequency")
plt.grid(axis='y')
plt.show()

# 3.3 Heatmap of User Activity by Location
activity_by_location = df.pivot_table(index='Location',
columns='Action', values='UserID', aggfunc='count', fill_value=0)
plt.figure(figsize=(12, 8))
sns.heatmap(activity_by_location, annot=True, fmt="d",
cmap="YlGnBu")
plt.title("User Activity by Location")
plt.xlabel("Action")
plt.ylabel("Location")
plt.show()

# 3.4 Failed Login Patterns Over Time
failed_logins = df[df['Action'] == 'Failed_Login']
failed_logins_over_time =
failed_logins.groupby(pd.Grouper(key='Timestamp', freq='D')).size()
plt.figure(figsize=(12, 6))
failed_logins_over_time.plot(color='red')
plt.title("Failed Login Attempts Over Time")
plt.xlabel("Date")
plt.ylabel("Failed Logins")
plt.grid()
plt.show()

# 3.5 Correlation Analysis
print("\nPerforming Correlation Analysis...")
aggregated_metrics['Failed_Login_Rate'] =
aggregated_metrics['Failed_Login_Rate'].fillna(0)
```

```
correlation_matrix = aggregated_metrics.corr()
plt.figure(figsize=(8, 6))
sns.heatmap(correlation_matrix, annot=True, cmap="coolwarm",
fmt='.2f')
plt.title("Correlation Matrix")
plt.show()

# Save cleaned and aggregated data for further analysis
cleaned_data_path = "Cleaned_Security_Data.csv"
df.to_csv(cleaned_data_path, index=False)
print(f"\nCleaned data saved to {cleaned_data_path}")
```

This Python program implements the steps outlined for **data preprocessing** and **exploratory data analysis (EDA)** on a synthetic security dataset:

1. Data Loading
- Reads the dataset containing user activities, such as logins, file access, and configuration changes, with associated metadata like timestamps, IP addresses, and locations.

2. Data Cleaning
- Removes duplicate rows and rows with missing essential fields (e.g. UserID, Timestamp).
- Normalizes fields like IP_Address and Resource for consistency.
- Converts timestamps to a datetime format for time-based analysis.

3. Feature Aggregation
- Derives new metrics such as:
    - **Session Duration**: Time spent by a user in the system (placeholder values used in the absence of logout timestamps).
    - **Failed Login Rate**: Ratio of failed login attempts to total login attempts per user.
    - **Action Count**: Total number of actions performed by each user.

4. Exploratory Data Analysis (EDA)
- **Visualization**:
    - **Login Frequency Distribution**: Displays how frequently users log in.
    - **Session Duration Distribution**: Highlights the range of session lengths.

- o **User Activity by Location**: A heatmap showing action counts across locations (e.g. HQ, Branch_Office).
- o **Failed Login Trends**: Plots failed login attempts over time to detect spikes or patterns.

- **Correlation Analysis**:
  - o Evaluates relationships between aggregated metrics (e.g. failed login rates and action counts) using a correlation heatmap.

5. Output
- Saves the cleaned and normalized dataset for further analysis.
- Provides visual and numerical insights into user behaviors and potential anomalies.

This program ensures the dataset is ready for advanced modelling and delivers actionable insights to inform security threat detection strategies. Let me know if you need further details or extensions!

6.2. Algorithm Selection and Justification

Choosing the right algorithm is critical to building an effective security threat detection system. This section discusses two major approaches: clustering for identifying anomalies in behavioral patterns and classification for detecting known threats. The strengths, limitations, and applications of each method are explored, along with Python code examples to demonstrate their implementation.

Clustering Algorithms

Clustering algorithms are unsupervised learning methods that group similar data points based on their features. They are particularly useful in scenarios where labeled data is unavailable, such as detecting unknown threats by identifying outlier behavior.

K-Means Clustering

- **Overview**: K-Means clustering partitions data into a predefined number of clusters, minimizing the variance within each cluster. It is suitable for grouping user behaviors, such as login frequencies or resource access patterns, and identifying users or sessions that fall outside normal clusters.
- **Use Case:**
  - o Group users based on typical activity patterns.

o Flag clusters with few members or high variance as potential anomalies.
- **Python Implementation**:

```python
from sklearn.cluster import KMeans
import matplotlib.pyplot as plt

# Data preparation (e.g. using aggregated metrics from
preprocessing)
features = aggregated_metrics[['Action_Count',
'Failed_Login_Rate']]

# Applying K-Means
kmeans = KMeans(n_clusters=3, random_state=42)
kmeans.fit(features)

# Adding cluster labels to the dataset
aggregated_metrics['Cluster'] = kmeans.labels_

# Visualizing Clusters
plt.figure(figsize=(10, 6))
for cluster in range(kmeans.n_clusters):
    cluster_data = features[aggregated_metrics['Cluster'] ==
cluster]
    plt.scatter(cluster_data['Action_Count'],
cluster_data['Failed_Login_Rate'], label=f'Cluster {cluster}')
plt.xlabel('Action Count')
plt.ylabel('Failed Login Rate')
plt.title('K-Means Clustering of User Behaviors')
plt.legend()
plt.show()
```

DBSCAN (Density-Based Spatial Clustering of Applications with Noise)
- **Overview**: DBSCAN is a density-based clustering algorithm that groups data points that are closely packed together while marking sparse regions as outliers. It is particularly effective for detecting anomalies in datasets with uneven densities.
- **Advantages**:
  - o Automatically identifies the number of clusters.
  - o Flags low-density areas as anomalies, which is valuable for detecting potential threats.
- **Python Implementation**:

```python
from sklearn.cluster import DBSCAN

# Data preparation (e.g. using aggregated metrics from
preprocessing)
features = aggregated_metrics[['Action_Count',
'Failed_Login_Rate']]

# Applying DBSCAN
dbscan = DBSCAN(eps=0.5, min_samples=5)
dbscan.fit(features)

# Adding cluster labels (-1 indicates noise) to the dataset
aggregated_metrics['DBSCAN_Cluster'] = dbscan.labels_

# Visualizing DBSCAN results
plt.figure(figsize=(10, 6))
for cluster in set(dbscan.labels_):
    cluster_data = features[aggregated_metrics['DBSCAN_Cluster'] ==
cluster]
    plt.scatter(cluster_data['Action_Count'],
cluster_data['Failed_Login_Rate'], label=f'Cluster {cluster}' if
cluster != -1 else 'Noise')
plt.xlabel('Action Count')
plt.ylabel('Failed Login Rate')
plt.title('DBSCAN Clustering of User Behaviors')
plt.legend()
plt.show()
```

Classification Algorithms

Classification algorithms are supervised learning methods used to categorize data based on labeled examples. These methods are effective for detecting known threats when historical data with labeled outcomes is available.

Gradient Boosting (e.g. XGBoost, LightGBM)

- **Overview**: Gradient Boosting algorithms build an ensemble of weak decision trees, iteratively improving their performance by minimizing prediction errors. They are highly accurate for tasks like identifying malicious activities based on predefined patterns.
- **Feature Importance**: Gradient Boosting models provide insights into which features contribute most to the predictions, aiding interpretability and feature selection.
- **Python Implementation**:

```python
from sklearn.model_selection import train_test_split
from xgboost import XGBClassifier
from sklearn.metrics import classification_report, roc_auc_score
import matplotlib.pyplot as plt

# Splitting the data into training and testing sets
X = aggregated_metrics[['Action_Count', 'Failed_Login_Rate']]
y = (aggregated_metrics['Failed_Login_Rate'] > 0.3).astype(int)   #
Example: High failed login rate as a threat
X_train, X_test, y_train, y_test = train_test_split(X, y,
test_size=0.2, random_state=42, stratify=y)

# Check if both classes are present in y_test
if len(set(y_test)) < 2:
    print("Warning: y_test contains only one class. ROC AUC Score
cannot be calculated.")
else:
    # Training an XGBoost classifier
    xgb_model = XGBClassifier(use_label_encoder=False,
eval_metric='logloss')
    xgb_model.fit(X_train, y_train)

    # Predictions and evaluation
    y_pred = xgb_model.predict(X_test)
    print(classification_report(y_test, y_pred))
    print(f"ROC AUC Score: {roc_auc_score(y_test, y_pred):.2f}")

    # Feature importance visualization
    importances = xgb_model.feature_importances_
    plt.figure(figsize=(8, 6))
    plt.bar(X.columns, importances, color='skyblue')
    plt.title('Feature Importance')
    plt.xlabel('Features')
    plt.ylabel('Importance Score')
    plt.show()
```

Criteria for Algorithm Selection

Choosing between clustering and classification depends on the nature of the data and the problem requirements:

Aspect	Clustering	Classification
Data Type	Unlabeled	Labeled
Use Case	Detecting unknown threats (anomalies).	Identifying known threats.
Algorithm Complexity	Generally simpler, but may need fine-tuning.	Moderate to complex, depending on the model.
Interpretability	Moderate (depends on the algorithm).	High (Gradient Boosting provides feature importance).

- **Decision-Making:**
  - o Use **Clustering** (e.g. K-Means, DBSCAN) for exploratory analysis and anomaly detection when no labels are available.
  - o Use **Classification** (e.g. Gradient Boosting) for predictive modelling when labeled historical data is available.

6.3 Implementation with Python

This section provides a comprehensive guide to implementing security threat detection using both clustering and classification algorithms. Each step is demonstrated with Python code, starting from data preprocessing to model evaluation.

Data Preprocessing

Before applying Machine Learning algorithms, the raw log data needs to be cleaned, normalized, and transformed into a format suitable for analysis.

Python Code for Data Preprocessing

```python
import pandas as pd
import numpy as np
from sklearn.preprocessing import StandardScaler

# Load the dataset
data_path = "Security_Threat_Dataset.csv"
df = pd.read_csv(data_path)
```

```python
# Data Cleaning
df.drop_duplicates(inplace=True)  # Remove duplicates
df = df.dropna(subset=['UserID', 'Timestamp'])  # Remove rows with
missing UserID or Timestamp
df['Timestamp'] = pd.to_datetime(df['Timestamp'])  # Convert
timestamps to datetime

# Feature Engineering
# Create a session duration placeholder
df['Session_Duration'] = np.where(df['Action'] == 'Logout',
np.random.randint(5, 120, size=len(df)), np.nan)

# Aggregated metrics
action_counts =
df.groupby('UserID')['Action'].count().rename('Action_Count')
failed_login_counts = df[df['Action'] ==
'Failed_Login'].groupby('UserID')['Action'].count()
failed_login_rate = (failed_login_counts /
action_counts).fillna(0).rename('Failed_Login_Rate')

# Combine into a single dataset
features = pd.concat([action_counts, failed_login_rate],
axis=1).reset_index()

# Normalize the data
scaler = StandardScaler()
scaled_features = scaler.fit_transform(features[['Action_Count',
'Failed_Login_Rate']])
features[['Action_Count', 'Failed_Login_Rate']] = scaled_features
```

Unsupervised Learning with Clustering

K-Means Clustering

K-Means is used to group similar behaviors and identify clusters with outlier's indicative of unusual activities.

```python
from sklearn.cluster import KMeans
import matplotlib.pyplot as plt

# Data preparation (e.g. using aggregated metrics from
preprocessing)
features = aggregated_metrics[['Action_Count',
'Failed_Login_Rate']]

from sklearn.cluster import KMeans
```

```python
import matplotlib.pyplot as plt

# Apply K-Means clustering
kmeans = KMeans(n_clusters=3, random_state=42)
features['Cluster'] = kmeans.fit_predict(features[['Action_Count',
'Failed_Login_Rate']])

# Visualize the clusters
plt.figure(figsize=(10, 6))
for cluster in range(kmeans.n_clusters):
    cluster_data = features[features['Cluster'] == cluster]
    plt.scatter(cluster_data['Action_Count'],
cluster_data['Failed_Login_Rate'], label=f'Cluster {cluster}')
plt.xlabel('Action Count')
plt.ylabel('Failed Login Rate')
plt.title('K-Means Clustering')
plt.legend()
plt.show()
```

Evaluating Clustering Performance

```python
from sklearn.metrics import silhouette_score, davies_bouldin_score

silhouette = silhouette_score(features[['Action_Count',
'Failed_Login_Rate']], features['Cluster'])
davies_bouldin = davies_bouldin_score(features[['Action_Count',
'Failed_Login_Rate']], features['Cluster'])

print(f"Silhouette Score: {silhouette:.2f}")
print(f"Davies-Bouldin Index: {davies_bouldin:.2f}")
```

The provided code evaluates the quality of clustering results using two metrics: the **Silhouette Score** and the **Davies-Bouldin Index**.

Key Components:
1. **Silhouette Score**:
    o **Definition**: Measures how similar an object is to its own cluster compared to other clusters.
    o **Range**: [-1, 1]
        ▪ **+1**: Perfectly clustered (samples are far away from other clusters).
        ▪ **0**: Overlapping clusters.

- ▪ **-1**: Misclassified clusters.
  - ○ **Formula**:

$$S(i) = \frac{b(i) - a(i)}{\max(a(i), b(i))}$$

- ▪ a(i): Mean distance between a sample and all other points in the same cluster.
- ▪ b(i): Mean distance between a sample and all points in the nearest neighboring cluster.

2. **Davies-Bouldin Index**:
   - ○ **Definition**: Measures the average similarity ratio between each cluster and its most similar cluster.
   - ○ **Range**: [0, ∞)
     - ▪ **Lower Values**: Better clustering (clusters are well-separated and compact).
   - ○ **Formula**:

$$DB = \frac{1}{N} \sum_{i=1}^{N} \max_{j \neq i} \frac{\sigma_i + \sigma_j}{d(c_i, c_j)}$$

- ▪ σi: Average distance of all points in cluster iii to the centroid of iii.
- ▪ d(ci,cj): Distance between the centroids of clusters iii and jjj.

- Silhouette score for the clustering, indicating the separation and cohesion of clusters.
  - ○ A higher value (closer to 1) indicates well-defined clusters.
- Davies-Bouldin Index, measuring the compactness and separation of clusters.
  - ○ A lower value indicates better clustering (clusters are compact and far apart).

These metrics are commonly used to evaluate clustering results in unsupervised learning tasks, helping you determine the quality of the clustering structure.

Supervised Learning with Gradient Boosting

Gradient Boosting Implementation

Gradient Boosting is applied to classify users based on labeled threat data.

```
from sklearn.model_selection import train_test_split
from xgboost import XGBClassifier
from sklearn.metrics import classification_report, roc_auc_score

# Data preparation (e.g. using aggregated metrics from
preprocessing)
features = aggregated_metrics[['Action_Count',
'Failed_Login_Rate']]


# Simulate labels: 1 for high failed login rate, 0 for normal
behavior
features['Threat'] = (features['Failed_Login_Rate'] >
0.5).astype(int)

# Train-test split
X = features[['Action_Count', 'Failed_Login_Rate']]
y = features['Threat']
X_train, X_test, y_train, y_test = train_test_split(X, y,
test_size=0.2, random_state=42)

# Train XGBoost model
xgb_model = XGBClassifier(use_label_encoder=False,
eval_metric='logloss')
xgb_model.fit(X_train, y_train)

# Predictions
y_pred = xgb_model.predict(X_test)
```

Evaluating Classification Performance

```
from sklearn.metrics import confusion_matrix, RocCurveDisplay

# Check if both classes are present in y_test
if len(set(y_test)) < 2:
    print("Warning: y_test contains only one class. ROC AUC Score
cannot be calculated.")
else:
    # Metrics
    print(classification_report(y_test, y_pred))
    roc_auc = roc_auc_score(y_test, y_pred)
    print(f"ROC AUC Score: {roc_auc:.2f}")

    # Confusion Matrix
```

```
    conf_matrix = confusion_matrix(y_test, y_pred)
    plt.figure(figsize=(6, 4))
    sns.heatmap(conf_matrix, annot=True, fmt='d', cmap='Blues',
xticklabels=['Normal', 'Threat'], yticklabels=['Normal', 'Threat'])
    plt.title('Confusion Matrix')
    plt.xlabel('Predicted')
    plt.ylabel('Actual')
    plt.show()
```

Metrics in the Report:
- **Precision**: Fraction of correct positive predictions out of all positive predictions.
- **Recall**: Fraction of correctly identified positive cases out of all actual positives.
- **F1-Score**: Harmonic mean of precision and recall.
- **Support**: Number of actual occurrences of each class in y_test.

ROC AUC Score:
- **Purpose**: Measures the model's ability to distinguish between classes.
- **Range**: [0, 1]
  - **0.5**: No discriminative ability (random guessing).
  - **1.0**: Perfect distinction between classes.
- **Calculation**: Based on the area under the Receiver Operating Characteristic (ROC) curve, which plots the true positive rate (TPR) vs. false positive rate (FPR).

6.4 Insights and Results

Clustering is a powerful tool for detecting anomalies in behavioral data by grouping similar patterns and identifying outliers. Visualizing clustering results is crucial for interpreting these groupings and understanding the nature of anomalies. This section explores the use of scatter plots and heatmaps to illustrate clustering results and analyze their implications.

Scatter Plots of Clusters

Scatter plots provide a two-dimensional representation of clusters based on key behavioral features. These visualizations help in identifying distinct clusters and spotting outliers that may indicate potential threats.
Purpose:
- To visualize how users or behaviors are grouped based on their similarities.

- To identify outlier clusters that deviate significantly from normal behavior.

Python Implementation:

```python
import matplotlib.pyplot as plt

# Scatter plot for K-Means Clustering
plt.figure(figsize=(10, 6))
for cluster in range(kmeans.n_clusters):
    cluster_data = features[features['Cluster'] == cluster]
    plt.scatter(cluster_data['Action_Count'],
cluster_data['Failed_Login_Rate'], label=f'Cluster {cluster}')

# Highlighting the plot
plt.xlabel('Action Count')
plt.ylabel('Failed Login Rate')
plt.title('K-Means Clustering of User Behaviors')
plt.legend()
plt.grid(True)
plt.show()
```

Insights:
1. **Cluster Separation**:
   - Distinct clusters suggest clear groupings of behaviors.
   - Well-separated clusters indicate that the features effectively represent user activity.

2. **Outlier Identification**:
   - Smaller clusters or points located far from the main clusters often represent unusual or suspicious behaviors.
   - For example, a user with an abnormally high failed login rate might form a separate cluster.

Heatmaps for Feature Analysis

Heatmaps are an excellent tool for analyzing the characteristics of clusters. By aggregating features within each cluster, heatmaps provide a detailed view of cluster behaviors and highlight deviations.

Purpose:
- To compare feature distributions across clusters.

- To detect patterns within clusters that may indicate normal or abnormal behavior.

Python Implementation:

```
import seaborn as sns

# Aggregate features by cluster for visualization
cluster_features = features.groupby('Cluster').mean()

# Heatmap
plt.figure(figsize=(12, 8))
sns.heatmap(cluster_features, annot=True, cmap="YlGnBu", fmt=".2f")
plt.title('Cluster Feature Analysis')
plt.xlabel('Features')
plt.ylabel('Cluster')
plt.show()
```

Insights:
1. **Feature Contribution**:
    - Heatmaps reveal which features are dominant in each cluster. For example, a cluster with high failed login rates and low action counts might represent threat behavior.
2. **Behavioral Patterns**:
    - Patterns within clusters help differentiate between normal and anomalous behaviors.

Analyzing Outlier Clusters
Clusters containing very few members or extreme values often signify anomalies. These clusters are critical for identifying security threats.

Analysis:
- **Small Clusters**:
    - Represent behaviors that differ significantly from the majority, such as a user accessing resources during unusual hours or an IP address with repeated failed logins.

- **Extreme Feature Values**:
  - o High values for features like failed login rates or action counts suggest suspicious activity, such as brute force login attempts or insider threats.

Case Study Example:
- **Outlier Cluster Analysis**:
  - o Cluster 2 contains only three users, each with a failed login rate exceeding 0.8 (80% of login attempts failed). This cluster is flagged for further investigation as it indicates repeated unauthorized access attempts.

Benefits of Clustering Visualization
1. **Intuitive Understanding**:
   - o Visual tools like scatter plots and heatmaps make complex clustering results accessible to non-technical stakeholders.
2. **Actionable Insights**:
   - o Outlier clusters provide immediate targets for further security analysis.
3. **Model Validation**:
   - o Visualization helps validate the clustering model by revealing how well it separates behaviors.

6.5 Classification Model Performances

Evaluating the performance of a classification model is critical to ensuring its effectiveness in identifying security threats. In the context of security threat detection, the model must accurately differentiate between normal and malicious behaviors while minimizing false positives and negatives. This section explores the performance of a Gradient Boosting model using various evaluation metrics, visualizations, and case analyses to understand its strengths and limitations.

Evaluation Metrics

To assess the classification model's performance, we use a combination of standard metrics:
1. **Precision**:
   - o Measures the proportion of correctly identified threats out of all predictions labeled as threats.
   - o High precision reduces the occurrence of false alarms.

Formula:

$$Precision = \frac{TP}{TP + FP}$$, where TP is true positives and FP is false positives.

2. **Recall:**
    o Measures the proportion of actual threats correctly identified by the model.
    o High recall ensures that most threats are captured.

Formula:

$$Recall = \frac{TP}{TP + FN}$$, where FN is false negatives.

3. **F1-Score:**
    o Harmonic mean of precision and recall, balancing both metrics.

Formula:

$$F1 = 2 \cdot \frac{Precision \cdot Recall}{Precision + Recall}$$

4. **ROC-AUC (Receiver Operating Characteristic - Area Under Curve):**
    o Evaluates the model's ability to distinguish between classes at various threshold levels.
    o A higher AUC indicates better overall performance.

Python Implementation for Metrics:

```python
from sklearn.metrics import classification_report, roc_auc_score

# Print classification report
print("Classification Report:")
print(classification_report(y_test, y_pred))

# Calculate and display ROC-AUC score
roc_auc = roc_auc_score(y_test, y_pred)
print(f"ROC-AUC Score: {roc_auc:.2f}")
```

Visualizing Performance

Visualization provides an intuitive understanding of the model's performance and helps stakeholders grasp key insights.

Confusion Matrix:

A confusion matrix breaks down predictions into four categories:

- **True Positives (TP)**: Correctly identified threats.
- **True Negatives (TN)**: Correctly identified normal behaviors.
- **False Positives (FP)**: Normal behaviors misclassified as threats.
- **False Negatives (FN)**: Threats missed by the model.

Python Implementation:

```python
from sklearn.metrics import confusion_matrix
import seaborn as sns
import matplotlib.pyplot as plt

# Generate confusion matrix
conf_matrix = confusion_matrix(y_test, y_pred)

# Visualize the confusion matrix
plt.figure(figsize=(8, 6))
sns.heatmap(conf_matrix, annot=True, fmt='d', cmap='Blues',
xticklabels=['Normal', 'Threat'], yticklabels=['Normal',
'Threat'])
plt.title('Confusion Matrix')
plt.xlabel('Predicted Class')
plt.ylabel('Actual Class')
plt.show()
```

Insights:

- **False Positives**:
    - o High false positives indicate over-sensitivity, leading to unnecessary alerts.
- **False Negatives**:
    - o High false negatives suggest the model is missing critical threats, which is a serious issue in security contexts.

ROC Curve:
The ROC curve plots the true positive rate (recall) against the false positive rate, showing the trade-off between sensitivity and specificity.

Python Implementation:

```
from sklearn.metrics import RocCurveDisplay

# Plot the ROC curve
plt.figure(figsize=(8, 6))
RocCurveDisplay.from_estimator(xgb_model, X_test, y_test)
plt.title('ROC Curve')
plt.show()
```

Insights:
- A curve closer to the top-left corner indicates a better-performing model.
- The area under the curve (AUC) provides a single metric summarizing the model's ability to classify threats.

Analysis of Model Predictions
Understanding how the model performs across different categories provides actionable insights for improvement:
1. **False Positives (FP):**
     - o Example: A user flagged as a threat due to high failed login rates but later verified to be an internal user with a temporary issue.
     - o Impact: False positives create alert fatigue and can divert attention from real threats.
2. **False Negatives (FN):**
     - o Example: A compromised account with minimal failed login attempts but accessing sensitive resources undetected.
     - o Impact: False negatives pose significant risks as they allow threats to go unnoticed.
3. **Correct Predictions:**
     - o Example: A malicious IP address repeatedly attempting logins and flagged correctly by the model.
     - o Impact: Correct predictions validate the model's effectiveness in identifying true threats.

6.6 Case Studies

Case studies are an essential part of understanding how a threat detection model performs in real-world scenarios. They provide practical insights into the model's behavior when identifying potential security breaches and help assess its reliability in diverse situations. This section examines specific examples of flagged activities, evaluates their significance, and discusses the outcomes of model predictions.

Case Study 1: Repeated Failed Login Attempts
Scenario:
A user was flagged by the model for an unusually high failed login rate. This user's actions were grouped into a distinct cluster by the K-Means algorithm, and the Gradient Boosting model classified the user as a potential threat.
Details:
- **Behavior:**
    - The user attempted to log in 50 times within a 10-minute window.
    - The failed login rate was 90%, far exceeding the average for other users.
    - IP address: 192.168.12.45.
    - Geolocation: Logged in from a location not typically associated with the user.
- **Model Interpretation:**
    - **Clustering:**
        - The K-Means algorithm grouped this behavior into an outlier cluster due to its deviation from normal patterns.
    - **Classification:**
        - Gradient Boosting flagged the user based on the high failed login rate.

Outcome:
- Investigation revealed that this was a brute force attack from an external IP address attempting to guess the user's password.
- Mitigation steps included blocking the IP address and implementing multi-factor authentication (MFA) for the user account.

Case Study 2: Unusual Resource Access Patterns
Scenario:
A user with regular login behavior was flagged for accessing sensitive resources repeatedly during non-business hours. The activity was identified as an anomaly by the clustering algorithm.

Details:
- **Behavior:**
  - The user accessed a confidential database (Database_1) 15 times between 1:00 AM and 3:00 AM.
  - No prior access to this database was recorded for this user.
  - Location: HQ.
- **Model Interpretation:**
  - **Clustering:**
    - DBSCAN marked this activity as an outlier due to its low density in the dataset.
  - **Classification:**
    - The Gradient Boosting model identified this user as a potential threat, based on resource access patterns and the time of access.

Outcome:
- Investigation revealed that the account had been compromised, and the attacker was exfiltrating data.
- Immediate actions included locking the account, notifying the user, and conducting a forensic analysis to identify the breach's scope.

Case Study 3: False Positive - High Failed Login Rate

Scenario:
The model flagged an internal user as a potential threat due to a high failed login rate, which was later determined to be a benign case.

Details:
- **Behavior:**
  - The user had 30 failed login attempts within 15 minutes.
  - The user's IP address and location were consistent with their usual activity.
- **Model Interpretation:**
  - **Clustering:**
    - K-Means placed the user in a cluster with high failed login rates, flagging it as suspicious.
  - **Classification:**
    - The Gradient Boosting model classified the user as a threat due to the failed login rate exceeding the threshold.

Outcome:
- Investigation revealed that the user had forgotten their password and repeatedly entered incorrect credentials.

- No malicious intent was detected.
- Actions included resetting the user's password and lowering the sensitivity of the failed login rate threshold for internal users.

Case Study 4: Normal User Activity
Scenario:
A user's behavior was classified as normal, demonstrating the model's ability to avoid over-flagging.
Details:
- **Behavior**:
  - Logged in 5 times during the day with no failed login attempts.
  - Accessed resources (File_1, File_2) consistent with their role.
  - IP address and location matched the user's profile.
- **Model Interpretation**:
  - **Clustering**:
    - K-Means grouped this behavior into a cluster representing typical activity.
  - **Classification**:
    - Gradient Boosting classified the user as normal with high confidence.

Outcome:
- No further investigation was required.
- The user's behavior served as a baseline for normal activity in future analyses.

Insights from Case Studies
1. **Model Strengths**:
   - Successfully identified critical threats such as brute force attacks and data exfiltration.
   - Flagged unusual behaviors for further investigation, reducing reliance on manual log analysis.
2. **False Positives**:
   - Highlighted areas for improvement, such as refining thresholds for internal users to reduce unnecessary alerts.
3. **Model Interpretability**:
   - Clustering provided intuitive groupings of behavior, making it easier to spot anomalies.
   - Gradient Boosting's feature importance scores helped justify classification decisions.

Generalization of Findings

Case studies demonstrate the real-world applicability of the threat detection system. Key lessons include:

- **Importance of Multi-Layer Detection**:
  - o Combining clustering and classification enhances reliability by addressing both known and unknown threats.
- **Role of Threshold Tuning**:
  - o Adjusting thresholds based on user roles and historical patterns reduces false positives.
- **Continuous Improvement**:
  - o Incorporating feedback from false positives and negatives into the model improves its adaptability.

* * *

Proactive Problem Management
With Predictive Insights

CHAPTER 7

PROACTIVE PROBLEM MANAGEMENT WITH PREDICTIVE INSIGHTS

Proactive problem management is a transformative approach in IT service management (ITSM) that focuses on identifying and resolving potential issues before they escalate into significant disruptions. Unlike reactive problem management, which deals with incidents after they occur, proactive problem management leverages predictive insights and data-driven methodologies to anticipate and mitigate problems, ensuring smooth operations and enhanced service reliability.

7.1 Overview of Proactive Problem Management

In traditional IT environments, problem management often operates in a reactive mode, where teams address incidents only after they have caused disruptions. While reactive management is essential for incident resolution, it is not sufficient to prevent recurring issues or predict future problems. This is where proactive problem management comes into play.

Key Characteristics of Proactive Problem Management:
1. **Anticipation of Issues**:
    o Identifies patterns and trends in historical data to forecast potential problems.
2. **Prevention**:
    o Implements measures to address root causes before incidents occur.
3. **Continuous Monitoring**:
    o Uses real-time data analysis to detect early warning signs of issues.

Benefits:
- **Reduced Downtime**:
    o By addressing issues before they escalate, organizations experience fewer service disruptions.

- **Cost Savings**:
  - Preventing problems is often less expensive than resolving them post-occurrence.
- **Improved Customer Satisfaction**:
  - Proactive problem management ensures higher service reliability, leading to better user experiences.

Role of Predictive Insights

Predictive insights form the backbone of proactive problem management. By analyzing historical and real-time data, organizations can identify patterns, predict potential issues, and implement preventative measures.

What are Predictive Insights?

Predictive insights involve using advanced analytics techniques, including Machine Learning (ML) and artificial intelligence (AI), to forecast future events based on past and current data.

Applications in IT Operations:

1. **Incident Prediction**:
   - Predicting the likelihood of recurring incidents based on historical logs.
   - Example: Forecasting server downtimes due to recurring high CPU utilization.
2. **Capacity Planning**:
   - Anticipating resource shortages to optimize infrastructure.
   - Example: Predicting storage exhaustion or bandwidth bottlenecks.
3. **Anomaly Detection**:
   - Identifying deviations from normal behavior to flag potential threats.
   - Example: Detecting unusual network traffic patterns indicating a possible DDoS attack.
4. **Root Cause Analysis**:
   - Clustering similar incidents to pinpoint underlying causes and address them proactively.

Key Technologies Driving Predictive Insights:

- **Machine Learning Models**:
  - Regression models, neural networks, and ensemble methods for predictive analytics.

- **Time-Series Analysis**:
    - ○ Techniques like ARIMA or LSTM for forecasting trends in resource utilization or incident occurrence.
- **Real-Time Monitoring Tools**:
    - ○ Systems like Splunk or Elastic Stack to gather and analyze live data streams.

Why Proactive Problem Management is the Future

As IT environments grow increasingly complex, the need for proactive problem management becomes more evident. Traditional reactive approaches are no longer sufficient to meet the demands of high-availability systems, rapid digital transformation, and escalating cyber threats.

Drivers of Proactive Problem Management:
- **Big Data**:
    - ○ The exponential growth of log and monitoring data necessitates advanced analytics to derive meaningful insights.
- **Machine Learning Advancements**:
    - ○ Improved algorithms and computational power enable real-time predictions with higher accuracy.
- **User Expectations**:
    - ○ End-users demand seamless experiences, making proactive service reliability a competitive advantage.

This chapter sets the stage for a deeper dive into the methodologies, tools, and techniques required to harness predictive insights for proactive problem management, providing a roadmap for IT organizations aiming to enhance their service capabilities.

7.2 Data Collection and Preprocessing

Effective data collection and preprocessing form the foundation for building robust predictive models for proactive problem management. This section explores the types of data required, the preprocessing steps to transform raw data into actionable insights, and the challenges encountered during this process.

Types of Data

Proactive problem management relies on diverse data sources that provide a comprehensive view of system performance, user activities, and historical incidents. The key types of data include:

1. **Incident Logs**:
   - Records of past incidents, including timestamps, affected resources, users involved, and resolution times.
   - Examples: Application errors, system crashes, or hardware failures.
2. **Service Requests**:
   - Data from ticketing systems detailing user-reported issues or requests for changes.
   - Examples: User complaints about slow system performance or requests for software upgrades.
3. **System Performance Metrics**:
   - Real-time and historical data on system health, such as CPU usage, memory consumption, and disk utilization.
   - Examples: Sudden spikes in CPU usage indicating potential overloads.
4. **Network Activity Logs**:
   - Logs of network traffic, including source and destination IPs, packet sizes, and transfer speeds.
   - Examples: Unusual network traffic patterns indicating potential DDoS attacks.
5. **Historical Problem Data**:
   - Records of recurring issues, root causes, and previous mitigation strategies.
   - Examples: Chronic database connection errors and their associated resolutions.

Why These Data Types Are Crucial:
- Incident logs and service requests help identify patterns of recurring issues.
- System performance metrics and network activity logs enable early detection of anomalies.
- Historical problem data provides context for root cause analysis and mitigation.

Datasets used:
- Incident_Analysis_Dataset.csv:
- Incident_Logs
- Network_Logs

Data Preprocessing

Raw data collected from diverse sources often requires extensive preprocessing to make it suitable for analysis and modelling. The key preprocessing steps include:

1. **Data Cleaning**:
    - **Removing Duplicates**:
        - Example: Eliminate repeated incident logs caused by redundant monitoring systems.
    - **Handling Missing Values**:
        - Use imputation techniques to fill gaps in data, such as estimating missing resolution times using median values.

Python Example:

```python
import pandas as pd
df = pd.read_csv("Proactive_Problem_Management_Dataset.csv")
# Remove duplicates
df.drop_duplicates(inplace=True)

# Handle missing values
df['ResolutionTime'] =
df['ResolutionTime'].fillna(df['ResolutionTime'].median(skipna=True
))
'''
skipna=True: Ensures that the .median() method ignores NaN values
when calculating the median.
'''
```

Normalization:

- Standardize metrics like resolution time or anomaly scores to ensure consistency.
- Example: Scale resolution times to a 0–1 range for comparison across incidents.

Python Example:

```python
from sklearn.preprocessing import MinMaxScaler

scaler = MinMaxScaler()
df['NormalizedResolutionTime'] =
scaler.fit_transform(df[['ResolutionTime']])
```

Feature Extraction:
- Derive new features from raw data to enrich the dataset:
  - **Incident Frequency**:
    - Calculate the number of incidents per resource or user within a given timeframe.
  - **Average Resolution Time**:
    - Compute the mean resolution time for recurring incidents.

Python Example:

```python
# Incident frequency per resource
incident_frequency =
df.groupby('Resource').size().rename('IncidentFrequency')

# Average resolution time for recurring incidents
avg_resolution_time =
df[df['Recurring']].groupby('Resource')['ResolutionTime'].mean().re
name('AvgResolutionTime')

# Merge back into the main dataset
df = df.merge(incident_frequency, on='Resource', how='left')
df = df.merge(avg_resolution_time, on='Resource', how='left')
```

Data Aggregation:
- Combine individual log entries into higher-level metrics:
  - Total incidents per resource or user.
  - Weekly or monthly incident trends.

Python Example:

```python
# Aggregating data into weekly incident trends
# Ensure 'Timestamp' is in datetime format
df['Timestamp'] = pd.to_datetime(df['Timestamp'], errors='coerce')

# Extract the ISO calendar week
df['Week'] = df['Timestamp'].dt.isocalendar().week


weekly_incidents =
df.groupby('Week').size().rename('WeeklyIncidents')
```

Challenges in Data Preparation

Data preparation for proactive problem management often faces several challenges:

1. **Handling Missing or Incomplete Data:**
    - **Challenge:**
        - Logs or metrics may be incomplete due to system failures or inconsistent monitoring configurations.
    - **Solution:**
        - Employ data imputation techniques, such as filling missing values with mean or median, or using Machine Learning models to predict missing entries.

Example:

```python
# Predict missing anomaly scores using a regression model
from sklearn.linear_model import LinearRegression

train_data = df.dropna(subset=['AnomalyScore'])
test_data = df[df['AnomalyScore'].isna()]

model = LinearRegression()
print(train_data.columns)
print(test_data[['IncidentFrequency', 'AvgResolutionTime']])
model.fit(train_data[['IncidentFrequency', 'AvgResolutionTime']],
train_data['AnomalyScore'])

df.loc[df['AnomalyScore'].isna(), 'AnomalyScore'] =
model.predict(test_data[['IncidentFrequency',
'AvgResolutionTime']])
```

Ensuring Data Privacy and Compliance:

- **Challenge:**
    - Incident logs and user data often contain sensitive information that must be protected to comply with regulations like GDPR or HIPAA.
- **Solution:**
    - Anonymize sensitive data fields (e.g. user IDs, IP addresses) while retaining their analytical value.

```
# Hash User IDs for anonymization
import hashlib

df['AnonymizedUserID'] = df['UserID'].apply(lambda x:
hashlib.sha256(x.encode()).hexdigest())
df.drop(columns=['UserID'], inplace=True)
```

Combining Data from Multiple Sources:
- **Challenge**:
  - ○ Integrating data from disparate systems (e.g. incident logs and network activity logs) with inconsistent formats and schemas.
- **Solution**:
  - ○ Standardize data formats and use keys like timestamps or resource identifiers for merging.
  - ○

```
# Merge incident logs and network activity logs on timestamp
incident_logs = pd.read_csv("incident_logs.csv")
network_logs = pd.read_csv("network_logs.csv")
combined_df = pd.merge(incident_logs, network_logs, on='Timestamp',
how='outer')
```

The data collection and preprocessing phase is foundational for proactive problem management. By consolidating and transforming diverse data sources—incident logs, service requests, system performance metrics, and more—into actionable datasets, organizations can unlock predictive insights and improve their IT operations. Overcoming challenges such as missing data and ensuring compliance requires careful planning and advanced techniques, paving the way for accurate modelling and impactful decision-making.

3. Predictive Analytics for Problem Management

Predictive analytics plays a pivotal role in proactive problem management by leveraging data-driven techniques to anticipate and mitigate potential issues. This section explores key techniques, Machine Learning models, and the importance of integrating domain expertise to enhance predictions.

Key Techniques

Predictive analytics relies on a combination of statistical and Machine Learning techniques to uncover patterns in data, identify anomalies, and predict future occurrences. The following techniques are particularly relevant for problem management:

Time-Series Forecasting

- **Purpose**:
  Predict recurring incidents or trends over time by analyzing historical data.
  Example: Forecasting spikes in CPU usage to prevent system overload.
- **Methods**:
  - **ARIMA (AutoRegressive Integrated Moving Average)**:
    - Suitable for linear time-series data.
  - **Prophet**:
    - Handles seasonality and trends with minimal configuration.
  - **LSTM (Long Short-Term Memory)**:
    - A neural network-based approach for capturing long-term dependencies in time-series data.

Anomaly Detection

- **Purpose**:
  Identify unusual patterns in data that may indicate potential issues or threats.
  Example: Detecting a sudden surge in network traffic indicative of a DDoS attack.
- **Methods**:
  - **Isolation Forest**:
    - Identifies anomalies based on data isolation.
  - **Autoencoders**:
    - Neural networks that learn to reconstruct input data, with reconstruction errors indicating anomalies.

Clustering

- **Purpose**:
  Group similar problems to facilitate root cause analysis and identify common issues.
- Example: Clustering incidents based on their types and severities to uncover systemic issues.

- **Methods:**
  - **K-Means:**
    - Groups data into a predefined number of clusters.
  - **DBSCAN:**
    - Identifies clusters in datasets with varying densities.

4. Implementation with Python

The Python implementation includes:

Data Preparation

- Normalization of numerical features like Resolution Time and Anomaly Score.
- Aggregating data into weekly counts for time-series forecasting.

Time-Series Forecasting

- Uses ARIMA to predict weekly incident counts.
- Visualizes historical data and forecasts.

Anomaly Detection

- Applies Isolation Forest to detect anomalies in Resolution Time and Anomaly Score.
- Visualizes anomalies using a scatter plot.

Root Cause Analysis

- Implements K-Means clustering to group incidents based on incident type and severity.
- Visualizes clusters to identify patterns.

Model Evaluation

- Metrics:
  - **ARIMA:** Mean Squared Error (MSE) for forecast evaluation.
  - **Isolation Forest:** Number of anomalies detected.
  - **K-Means:** Cluster distribution for analyzing root causes.

Code:

```
import pandas as pd
import numpy as np
import matplotlib.pyplot as plt
import seaborn as sns
from sklearn.preprocessing import StandardScaler
from sklearn.ensemble import IsolationForest
from sklearn.metrics import mean_squared_error,
classification_report
from statsmodels.tsa.arima.model import ARIMA
```

```python
from sklearn.cluster import KMeans

# Load dataset
data_path = "Incident_Analysis_Dataset.csv"
df = pd.read_csv(data_path)
df['Timestamp'] = pd.to_datetime(df['Timestamp'])

# 4.1 Data Preparation
# Feature Engineering: Create time-based features and normalize
numerical columns
print("Preparing Data...")
df['Week'] = df['Timestamp'].dt.isocalendar().week
df['DayOfWeek'] = df['Timestamp'].dt.dayofweek

scaler = StandardScaler()
df['NormalizedResolutionTime'] =
scaler.fit_transform(df[['ResolutionTime']])
df['NormalizedAnomalyScore'] =
scaler.fit_transform(df[['AnomalyScore']])

# Aggregating data by week for time-series forecasting
time_series_data = df.set_index('Timestamp').resample('W').size()
time_series_data.name = 'IncidentCount'
print("Data Preparation Complete")

# 4.2 Time-Series Forecasting with ARIMA
print("Performing Time-Series Forecasting...")
arima_model = ARIMA(time_series_data, order=(2, 1, 2))
model_fit = arima_model.fit()
forecast = model_fit.forecast(steps=12)

# Plot the results
plt.figure(figsize=(10, 6))
plt.plot(time_series_data, label='Historical Data')
plt.plot(forecast, label='Forecast', color='red')
plt.title('Weekly Incident Count Forecast')
plt.legend()
plt.show()

# Line chart for forecasted incidents and actual trends
plt.figure(figsize=(10, 6))
plt.plot(time_series_data[-24:], label='Actual Trends',
color='blue')
plt.plot(forecast, label='Forecasted Incidents', color='green',
linestyle='dashed')
plt.title('Forecasted Incidents vs Actual Trends')
plt.legend()
plt.show()
```

```
print("Forecast Complete")

# 4.3 Anomaly Detection with Isolation Forest
print("Performing Anomaly Detection...")
anomaly_features = df[['NormalizedResolutionTime',
'NormalizedAnomalyScore']]
isolation_forest = IsolationForest(contamination=0.05,
random_state=42)
df['AnomalyFlag'] = isolation_forest.fit_predict(anomaly_features)

# Visualize anomalies
plt.figure(figsize=(10, 6))
anomalies = df[df['AnomalyFlag'] == -1]
plt.scatter(df['ResolutionTime'], df['AnomalyScore'],
label='Normal', alpha=0.5)
plt.scatter(anomalies['ResolutionTime'], anomalies['AnomalyScore'],
label='Anomalies', color='red')
plt.xlabel('Resolution Time')
plt.ylabel('Anomaly Score')
plt.title('Anomaly Detection Results')
plt.legend()
plt.show()

# Heatmap for anomaly detection results
heatmap_data = pd.crosstab(df['DayOfWeek'], df['AnomalyFlag'],
normalize='index')
plt.figure(figsize=(8, 6))
sns.heatmap(heatmap_data, annot=True, cmap="coolwarm", fmt='.2f')
plt.title('Heatmap of Anomaly Detection by Day of Week')
plt.xlabel('Anomaly Flag (-1: Anomaly, 1: Normal)')
plt.ylabel('Day of Week')
plt.show()
print("Anomaly Detection Complete")

# 4.4 Root Cause Analysis with K-Means Clustering
print("Performing Clustering for Root Cause Analysis...")
clustering_features = pd.get_dummies(df[['IncidentType',
'Severity']])
kmeans = KMeans(n_clusters=5, random_state=42)
df['Cluster'] = kmeans.fit_predict(clustering_features)

# Visualize clusters
plt.figure(figsize=(10, 6))
for cluster in range(5):
    cluster_data = df[df['Cluster'] == cluster]
    plt.scatter(cluster_data.index, cluster_data['ResolutionTime'],
label=f'Cluster {cluster}')
plt.xlabel('Index')
```

```
plt.ylabel('Resolution Time')
plt.title('Clustering of Incidents')
plt.legend()
plt.show()
print("Clustering Complete")

# 4.5 Model Evaluation
print("Evaluating Models...")
# Evaluate ARIMA forecast
mse = mean_squared_error(time_series_data[-12:], forecast[:12])
print(f"ARIMA Mean Squared Error: {mse:.2f}")

# Evaluate Isolation Forest
print("Isolation Forest Results:")
print(f"Number of anomalies detected: {len(anomalies)}")

# Evaluate K-Means clustering
print("Cluster Distribution:")
print(df['Cluster'].value_counts())

print("Model Evaluation Complete")
```

5. Challenges and Considerations

Implementing predictive analytics for proactive problem management is a complex task that requires overcoming several challenges and making careful considerations. This section explores these challenges and provides strategies to address them effectively.

5.1. Data Challenges

5.1.1 Data Quality

- **Challenge**:
  Predictive models rely heavily on high-quality data. Missing, incomplete, or inconsistent data can lead to inaccurate predictions and unreliable insights.
- **Examples**:
  - o Missing resolution times in incident logs.
  - o Inconsistent formatting of timestamps across datasets.
- **Solution**:
  - o Implement robust data cleaning and preprocessing pipelines to handle missing values, standardize formats, and address inconsistencies.

  o Use imputation techniques, such as mean or median substitution, or predictive modelling to fill gaps.

5.1.2 Data Volume
- **Challenge**:
  Large-scale IT environments generate vast amounts of data from logs, metrics, and monitoring systems. Processing and analyzing such volumes can be computationally expensive.
- **Examples**:
  - o Logs with millions of entries for a high-traffic network.
  - o Real-time monitoring data from distributed systems.
- **Solution**:
  - o Use big data tools like Apache Spark or Hadoop to process large datasets.
  - o Implement sampling techniques for exploratory analysis and focus on critical features for modeling.

5.1.3 Data Relevance
- **Challenge**:
  Not all collected data is relevant for predictive analytics. Irrelevant features may introduce noise and reduce model performance.
- **Examples**:
  - o Logs with redundant information that do not contribute to problem prediction.
  - o Metrics with little correlation to incident occurrence.
- **Solution**:
  - o Conduct feature selection using techniques like correlation analysis, PCA (Principal Component Analysis), or domain expert input.
  - o Regularly review data pipelines to ensure relevance.

5.2. Modelling Challenges
5.2.1 Model Selection
- **Challenge**:
  Choosing the right model for the specific use case is critical. Different problems (e.g. anomaly detection, time-series forecasting) require different algorithms.

- **Examples**:
    - o Selecting between ARIMA, Prophet, or LSTM for time-series forecasting.
    - o Deciding between Isolation Forest or Autoencoders for anomaly detection.
- **Solution**:
    - o Conduct exploratory model trials and compare performance using metrics like MSE, F1-Score, or ROC-AUC.
    - o Consider model interpretability and scalability as part of the selection process.

5.2.2 Imbalanced Data

- **Challenge**:

  Security incidents and anomalies are often rare events, leading to imbalanced datasets that skew model predictions.
- **Examples**:
    - o A dataset with 95% normal incidents and 5% anomalies.
- **Solution**:
    - o Use techniques like oversampling (e.g. SMOTE) or undersampling to balance the dataset.
    - o Apply cost-sensitive learning to penalize misclassification of rare classes.

5.2.3 Model Generalization

- **Challenge**:

  Models trained on historical data may fail to generalize to new, unseen scenarios.
- **Examples**:
    - o A model that performs well on training data but fails to detect novel anomalies.
- **Solution**:
    - o Regularly update models with new data to ensure they capture evolving patterns.
    - o Use ensemble methods to combine multiple models for better generalization.

5.3. Operational Considerations

5.3.1 Integration with Existing Systems

- **Challenge:**
Predictive models must integrate seamlessly with existing ITSM workflows and tools.
- **Examples:**
  - Incorporating predictive insights into incident management platforms like ServiceNow.
- **Solution:**
  - Develop APIs or connectors to integrate models with ITSM tools.
  - Ensure the output is presented in an actionable format for IT teams.

5.3.2 Real-Time Processing

- **Challenge:**
Many predictive analytics applications require real-time analysis to provide timely insights.
- **Examples:**
  - Real-time anomaly detection for DDoS attacks.
- **Solution:**
  - Use streaming platforms like Apache Kafka or real-time analytics tools to process live data feeds.
  - Optimize model inference times for low-latency predictions.

5.3.3 False Positives and Negatives

- **Challenge:**
High false positive rates can overwhelm IT teams, while false negatives can lead to missed critical issues.
- **Examples:**
  - An anomaly detection model incorrectly flags normal activity as suspicious.
- **Solution:**
  - Fine-tune model thresholds based on domain knowledge and operational requirements.
  - Implement a feedback loop where flagged cases are reviewed and used to refine models.

5.4. Ethical and Privacy Considerations
5.4.1 Data Privacy
- **Challenge**:
  Predictive models often use sensitive data, such as user activity logs and network traffic, which must be handled in compliance with regulations.
- **Examples**:
  - GDPR or HIPAA requirements for data handling and storage.
- **Solution**:
  - Anonymize sensitive data fields, such as user IDs and IP addresses.
  - Ensure secure data storage and access controls.

5.4.2 Model Bias
- **Challenge**:
  Bias in training data can lead to biased predictions, disproportionately affecting certain users or systems.
- **Examples**:
  - A model that over-prioritizes incidents from high-traffic resources due to data imbalance.
- **Solution**:
  - Regularly audit models for biases.
  - Incorporate diverse and representative data during training.

5.5. Maintenance and Scalability
5.5.1 Continuous Monitoring and Updates
- **Challenge**:
  Predictive models degrade over time as patterns in the data evolve.
- **Examples**:
  - A model trained on last year's data may not account for new configurations or policies.
- **Solution**:
  - Implement automated retraining pipelines to update models regularly.
  - Monitor model performance metrics to detect degradation early.

5.5.2 Scalability
- **Challenge**:
  As the organization grows, the volume and complexity of data increase, requiring scalable solutions.
- **Examples**:

- o   A sudden increase in the number of monitored resources or users.
- **Solution**:
    - o   Use cloud-based infrastructure to scale resources dynamically.
    - o   Optimize models for distributed processing.

Addressing the challenges and considerations outlined above is essential for successful implementation of predictive analytics in proactive problem management. By tackling data quality issues, selecting appropriate models, and integrating solutions into existing workflows, organizations can maximize the effectiveness of their predictive systems. Ethical considerations, such as data privacy and bias mitigation, ensure that these systems are both reliable and responsible, paving the way for robust and sustainable IT operations.

* * *

Comprehensive
IT Operations

CHAPTER 8

COMPREHENSIVE IT OPERATIONS

ANOMALY DETECTION IN A LOG FILE

Abnormalities in patterns or deviations from the expected norms are called anomalies. The data in itself may not be anomaly (if it is then would be classified as Point Anomaly) but given the context (other data/information) - Contextual Anomaly. This type of anomaly is common in time-series data.

Examples:
- A sudden surge in order volume at an eCommerce company, as seen in that company's hourly total orders for example, could be a contextual outlier if this high volume occurs outside of a known promotional discount or high-volume period like Black Friday. Could this stampede be due to a pricing glitch which is allowing customers to pay pennies on the dollar for a product?
- Spending $100 on food every day is odd but normal during the holiday season (given the context that it is the holiday season).

Some examples from IT Operations:
1. Unusual Spike in Login Attempts
- **Scenario**: A sudden surge in login attempts to a company's system during non-business hours.
- **Context**: If the company operates only during regular business hours, this surge could indicate a **brute force attack** or **credential stuffing** attempt, especially if the attempts are from a single IP or geographic region.
- **Explanation**: Without the context of business hours or known maintenance periods, this activity might seem benign.

2. Unexpected Increase in API Calls
- **Scenario**: A sharp increase in API calls to a payment gateway.
- **Context**: If the increase occurs outside of a known peak time (e.g. end-of-month billing cycles) or lacks a promotional event driving such traffic, it could indicate a **bot attack** or an API abuse situation.
- **Explanation**: The volume of requests itself isn't an anomaly but becomes one when contextualized with time and expected traffic patterns.

3. High Disk Usage on a Specific Server
- **Scenario**: A single server in a distributed system suddenly shows 95% disk usage.
- **Context**: If no backup process, large data transfer, or batch processing job is scheduled for that server, it might indicate a **memory leak**, **misconfigured logging**, or a **malicious data upload** attempt.
- **Explanation**: High disk usage might be routine during scheduled operations, but in this context, it's anomalous.

4. Network Traffic Spikes
- **Scenario**: A significant spike in outbound traffic from a server in a private network.
- **Context**: If this happens outside known data transfer schedules (e.g. daily backups or updates) it might indicate **data exfiltration** by malicious actors or a compromised system.
- **Explanation**: The traffic itself isn't anomalous, but the timing and absence of a valid trigger make it suspicious.

5. Sudden Drop in Application Response Time
- **Scenario**: The response time of a web application suddenly drops to near-instantaneous for a subset of users.
- **Context**: If this happens during peak load, it could be due to **failed logging**, **skipped validations**, or **load balancer misconfigurations** that bypass parts of the normal process.
- **Explanation**: A faster response might seem positive but could indicate a deeper system flaw when analyzed in context.

6. Sudden Surge in Error Logs
- **Scenario**: A sharp increase in error messages in a log file for a database query.
- **Context**: If no schema changes, application updates, or new feature rollouts have occurred, this could indicate an **SQL injection attempt**, **misconfiguration**, or **data corruption**.
- **Explanation**: Errors may not always signify anomalies, but their timing and frequency compared to regular operations make them context-specific anomalies.

7. CPU Spikes During Idle Periods
- **Scenario**: A CPU utilization spike of over 90% at midnight.

- **Context**: If no batch jobs, data analytics processes, or scheduled scans are configured during that time, it could indicate a **crypto-mining attack** or **malware activity**.
- **Explanation**: High CPU usage is typical for resource-intensive tasks, but its occurrence during idle periods raises flags.

8. Unexpected User Activity

- **Scenario**: An employee account downloads 10 GB of data at 3 a.m.
- **Context**: If the employee doesn't work night shifts and no bulk download permissions were granted, this could indicate **compromised credentials** or **insider data theft**.
- **Explanation**: Data download itself isn't unusual; the timing and user profile make it anomalous.

9. Frequent Service Restarts

- **Scenario**: A microservice in a Kubernetes cluster restarts 20 times in an hour.
- **Context**: If no deployment updates or system maintenance tasks are scheduled, this could suggest a **bug in the code**, **resource contention**, or **DoS attack** targeting the service.
- **Explanation**: Service restarts might be part of regular operations, but the frequency and timing are the anomalies.

10. Delayed Log File Updates

- **Scenario**: Log files for a critical application stop updating for an hour and then resume.
- **Context**: If there is no maintenance or downtime planned, this could indicate **application hangs**, **logging misconfigurations**, or an **interruption in system connectivity**.
- **Explanation**: Log updates resuming might hide the anomaly without considering the downtime context.

Contextual anomalies in IT operations highlight the importance of correlating time-series data with system knowledge, scheduled events, and expected behaviors. Proper monitoring tools and frameworks, such as the one proposed in the referenced paper, can identify these anomalies and prevent potential security or operational issues.

IMPLEMENTATION OF LOG ANALYSIS

This is based on the research paper: https://www.skopik.at/ait/2018_ispec.pdf
The paper titled **"Time Series Analysis: Unsupervised Anomaly Detection Beyond Outlier Detection"** presents a novel approach for identifying anomalies in log data, addressing challenges in traditional anomaly detection methods. The authors emphasize that static clustering and basic outlier detection methods are inadequate for dynamic systems, where cluster configurations and system behavior evolve over time. The proposed solution focuses on leveraging time-series analysis combined with dynamic clustering to provide a more robust and adaptive framework for anomaly detection.

Core Contributions

1. **Dynamic Clustering with Evolution Tracking**
    -   The authors introduce a technique to generate cluster maps that evolve over time, capturing changes such as transitions, splits, and merges in cluster configurations. This enables the detection of anomalies linked to structural shifts in log data.
    -   The dynamic nature of the clustering mechanism is particularly well-suited for real-world systems, where static models struggle to adapt to changing conditions.
2. **Anomaly Detection Beyond Outliers**
    -   Traditional anomaly detection methods often rely on identifying outliers as points that deviate from cluster centers. However, the paper proposes analyzing the **frequency** and **periodicity** of events within clusters to identify more subtle anomalies.
    -   This allows for the detection of both transient anomalies (e.g. a one-time outlier) and persistent, systemic changes in behavior.
3. **Unsupervised Learning Framework**
    -   The proposed method operates without the need for labeled datasets, making it highly adaptable to systems where labeled training data may not exist.
    -   This unsupervised approach is capable of identifying previously unseen types of anomalies, a critical capability for cybersecurity applications.

The steps are described in the research paper under Fig. 2:

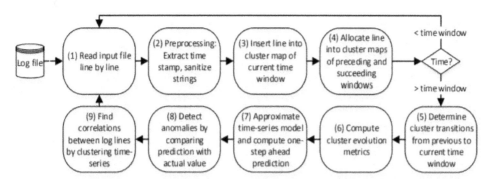

Steps we followed:
1. Parse log file, text preprocessing
2. Feature Engineering with word embedding model (ex. Word2Vec, BERT, Universal Sentence Encoder etc.)
3. Cluster log lines into k groups (K-Means etc.)
4. Determine cluster counts occurring within fixed time windows, t
5. Compute moving averages of cluster counts (or more robust models such as LSTM)
6. Forecast one-step ahead
7. Compute confidence interval for forecast and classify anomalies based on this interval

Dataset:
https://github.com/swapnilsaurav/ITOpExcellence/blob/main/logdata_full.txt

The primary goal of this project is to predict data patterns over time and analyze prediction errors. The project utilizes Machine Learning models and statistical analysis to evaluate performance and provide insights into prediction reliability.

Dataset Overview
- **Dataset Description**: The dataset appears to include time-series data used for prediction tasks. Specific details about the data source, features, and target variable are not included in the notebook but can be inferred from variable names and visualization.
- **Preprocessing**:
  - Data is visualized for both predicted and actual values.
  - Rolling window calculations are applied to compute moving averages and standard deviations for error analysis.

Program: Create a UI tool to convert Text File to CSV using Python

```python
import pandas as pd
read_file = pd.read_csv
(r'https://raw.githubusercontent.com/swapnilsaurav/ITOpExcellence/r
efs/heads/main/logdata_full.txt')
read_file.to_csv ('LogFileForAnalysis.csv', index=None)
print(read_file)


import tkinter as tk
from tkinter import filedialog
from tkinter import messagebox
import pandas as pd

root = tk.Tk()

canvas1 = tk.Canvas(root, width=300, height=300,
bg='lightsteelblue2', relief='raised')
canvas1.pack()

label1 = tk.Label(root, text='File Conversion Tool',
bg='lightsteelblue2')
label1.config(font=('helvetica', 20))
canvas1.create_window(150, 60, window=label1)

def getTxt():
    global read_file

    import_file_path = filedialog.askopenfilename()
    read_file = pd.read_csv(import_file_path)

browseButtonTxt = tk.Button(text="       Import Text File       ",
command=getTxt, bg='green', fg='white',
                            font=('helvetica', 12, 'bold'))
canvas1.create_window(150, 130, window=browseButtonTxt)

def convertToCsv():
    global read_file
    export_file_path =
filedialog.asksaveasfilename(defaultextension='.csv')
    read_file.to_csv(export_file_path, index=None)

saveAsButtonCsv = tk.Button(text='Convert Text to CSV',
command=convertToCsv, bg='green', fg='white',
                            font=('helvetica', 12, 'bold'))
canvas1.create_window(150, 180, window=saveAsButtonCsv)
```

```
def exitApplication():
    MsgBox = tk.messagebox.askquestion('Exit Application', 'Are you
sure you want to exit the application',icon='warning')
    if MsgBox == 'yes':
        root.destroy()

exitButton = tk.Button(root, text='        Exit Application        ',
command=exitApplication, bg='brown', fg='white',
                        font=('helvetica', 12, 'bold'))
canvas1.create_window(150, 230, window=exitButton)
root.mainloop()
```

Program 1: Create a UI tool to convert Text File to CSV using Python

Methodology

1. **Prediction Model**:
   - o The notebook utilizes a pre-trained prediction model (LSTM).
   - o Predictions are generated for a specified time period.
2. **Error Analysis**:
   - o Moving averages and standard deviations are calculated using rolling windows.
   - o Confidence intervals are constructed for 1-sigma, 2-sigma, and 3-sigma bounds, representing one, two, and three standard deviations from the mean.
3. **Visualization**:
   - o The predictions and actual values are plotted over time.
   - o Confidence intervals are shaded to visualize variability and prediction confidence.

Program: Now Read the csv file for performing Contextual Analysis

```
import nltk
nltk.download('punkt')
import pandas as pd
import numpy as np
df = pd.read_csv("C:/loganalysis/LogFileForAnalysis.csv")
```

	LineId	Date	Time	Pid	Level	Component	Content	EventId	EventTemplate
0	1	24-01-2122	00:00:00	143	INFO	dfs.DataNode\$DataXceiver	Receiving block blk_-1608999687919862906 src: ...	E5	Receiving block <*> src: /<*> dest: /<*>
1	2	24-01-2122	00:00:00	35	INFO	dfs.FSNamesystem	BLOCK* NameSystem.allocateBlock: /mnt/hadoop/m...	E22	BLOCK* NameSystem.allocateBlock: <*>
2	3	24-01-2122	00:00:01	143	INFO	dfs.DataNode\$DataXceiver	Receiving block blk_-1608999687919862906 src: ...	E5	Receiving block <*> src: /<*> dest: /<*>
3	4	24-01-2122	00:00:03	145	INFO	dfs.DataNode\$DataXceiver	Receiving block blk_-1608999687919862906 src: ...	E5	Receiving block <*> src: /<*> dest: /<*>
4	5	24-01-2122	00:00:06	145	INFO	dfs.DataNode\$PacketResponder	PacketResponder 1 for block blk_-1608999687919...	E11	PacketResponder <*> for block <*> terminating

```python
#1. Make the text file for word tokenization
import os

name_of_text_file = 'input.txt'

if name_of_text_file not in os.listdir(os.getcwd()):
    filedata = df['Content'] + " " + df['EventTemplate'] + " "

    s = [x for x in filedata]
    text = ''.join(s)
    text_file = open("input.txt", "w")
    text_file.write(text)
    text_file.close()

#2. Implementating Word2Vec Modelling
from nltk.tokenize import sent_tokenize, word_tokenize
import gensim
from tqdm import tqdm
sample = open('./input.txt', "r")
s = sample.read()

f = s.replace("\n", " ")
symbols = ['/', '<', '>', ':', '.', ':', '*'] # to filter out the symbols
data = []

for i in tqdm(sent_tokenize(f)):
    temp = []
    for j in word_tokenize(i):
        if j not in symbols:
            temp.append(j.lower())
    data.append(temp)

# Create CBOW model
model1 = gensim.models.Word2Vec(data, min_count = 1, size = 32, window = 5)
model1.most_similar('NameSystem.allocateBlock'.lower())

print(model1.similarity('NameSystem.allocateBlock'.lower(), 'succeeded'))
```

```python
#3. Now Make sentence vec
sen = df['Content'] + ' ' + df['EventTemplate']
sen2vec = []
for x in sen:
    for i in sent_tokenize(x):
        temp = []
        for j in word_tokenize(i):
            if j not in symbols:
                try:
                    temp.append(model1[j.lower()])
                except:
                    print(j)
    l = np.array(temp)
    l = np.average(l,axis=0)
    sen2vec.append(l)

sen2vec = np.array(sen2vec)
print(sen2vec)

#4. window generator
from datetime import datetime, timedelta


class DataGen:
    def __init__(self, time, window):
        self.time = time
        self.window = timedelta(minutes=window)
        self.index = 0
        self.start = datetime.strptime(self.time[0], "%H:%M:%S")
        self.it = 1

    def __iter__(self):
        return self

    def __next__(self):
        self.indextime = datetime.strptime(self.time[self.index],
"%H:%M:%S")
        for x in range(self.index, len(self.time)):
            temp = datetime.strptime(self.time[x], "%H:%M:%S")
            if temp - self.start >= self.window * self.it:
                self.index = x
                self.it += 1
                return self.index
        raise StopIteration


def extract_max_min(dic):
    max_value = -1
```

```
    min_value = 100000000
    for x in dic:
        if dic[x] > max_value:
            max_value = dic[x]
        if dic[x] < min_value:
            min_value = dic[x]
    return max_value, min_value

for x in DataGen(df["Time"], window=2):
    print(x)
    print(df["Time"][x])
    break

#Saving all columns to time window relations
itr = 0
dic_col_relation = {}
start = 0
for x in DataGen(df["Time"], window=2):
    dic_col_relation[itr] = {'start': start, 'end': x}
    start = x
    itr += 1

##Step 3 from the paper- Auto K mean algo
from sklearn.cluster import KMeans
from sklearn.metrics import silhouette_samples, silhouette_score
import matplotlib.pyplot as plt
import matplotlib.cm as cm
import numpy as np
from tqdm import tqdm

plt.style.use('ggplot')
training_file_name = 'k_values.npy'

if name_of_text_file not in os.listdir(os.getcwd()):
    range_n_clusters = [2, 3, 4, 5, 6, 7, 8, 9, 10, 11, 12, 13, 14,
15]

    k_values = []
    cluster_values = []

    start = 0
    for end in tqdm(DataGen(df["Time"], window=2)):
        X = sen2vec[start:end]
        start, end = end, _

        k_values_score = []
        clusters = []
        for n_clusters in range_n_clusters:
```

```
            clusterer = KMeans(n_clusters=n_clusters,
random_state=10)
            cluster_labels = clusterer.fit_predict(X)
            unique, counts = np.unique(cluster_labels,
return_counts=True)
            stats = dict(zip(unique, counts))
            max_value, min_value = extract_max_min(stats)
            clusters.append([max_value, min_value])
            silhouette_avg = silhouette_score(X, cluster_labels)
            k_values_score.append(silhouette_avg)

        i = np.argmax(k_values_score)
        k_value = range_n_clusters[i]
        max_value, min_value = clusters[i]
        cluster_values.append([max_value, min_value])
        k_values.append(k_value)

#https://scikit-
learn.org/stable/auto_examples/cluster/plot_kmeans_silhouette_analy
sis.html#sphx-glr-auto-examples-cluster-plot-kmeans-silhouette-
analysis-py

k_values = np.load('k_values.npy')
# load the result of training from k_values.npy file
cluster_values = np.load('cluster_values.npy')
from matplotlib.pyplot import figure
figure(num=None, figsize=(16, 8), dpi=80, facecolor='w',
edgecolor='k')
plt.plot(k_values, '-')
plt.title("time window 2 min")
plt.xlabel("time")
plt.ylabel("k-number")

############# Plot
```

```python
fig = figure(num=None, figsize=(16, 8), dpi=80)
plt.plot(cluster_values[:,0], '-', label='max')
plt.plot(cluster_values[:,1], '-', label='min')

plt.title("time window 2 min")
plt.xlabel("time")
plt.ylabel("cluster size")
plt.savefig("min_max_cluster_size")
plt.legend()
# Window
```

```python
### Building the Model
from pandas import DataFrame
from pandas import Series
from pandas import concat
from pandas import read_csv
from pandas import datetime
from sklearn.metrics import mean_squared_error
from sklearn.preprocessing import MinMaxScaler
from keras.models import Sequential
from keras.layers import Dense,Input
from keras.layers import LSTM
from keras import regularizers
from keras import optimizers
from math import sqrt

from keras.models import Model, load_model
def timeseries_to_supervised(data, lag=1):
    df = DataFrame(data)
    columns = [df.shift(i) for i in range(1, lag+1)]
    columns.append(df)
    df = concat(columns, axis=1)
    df.fillna(0, inplace=True)
```

```python
    return df
# create a differenced series
def difference(dataset, interval=1):
    diff = list()
    for i in range(interval, len(dataset)):
        value = dataset[i] - dataset[i - interval]
        diff.append(value)
    return Series(diff)


# invert differenced value
def inverse_difference(history, yhat, interval=1):
    return yhat + history[-interval]


# scale train and test data to [-1, 1]
def scale(train, test):
    # fit scaler
    scaler = MinMaxScaler(feature_range=(-1, 1))
    scaler = scaler.fit(train)
    # transform train
    train = train.reshape(train.shape[0], train.shape[1])
    train_scaled = scaler.transform(train)
    # transform test
    test = test.reshape(test.shape[0], test.shape[1])
    test_scaled = scaler.transform(test)
    return scaler, train_scaled, test_scaled


# inverse scaling for a forecasted value
def invert_scale(scaler, X, value):
    new_row = [x for x in X] + [value]
    array = np.array(new_row)
    array = array.reshape(1, len(array))
    inverted = scaler.inverse_transform(array)
    return inverted[0, -1]


# fit an LSTM network to training data
def fit_lstm(train, batch_size, nb_epoch, neurons):
    X, y = train[:, 0:-1], train[:, -1]
    X = X.reshape(X.shape[0], 1, X.shape[1])
    model = Sequential()
    model.add(LSTM(neurons, batch_input_shape=(batch_size,
X.shape[1], X.shape[2]), stateful=True))
    model.add(Dense(1))
    model.compile(loss='mean_squared_error', optimizer='adam')
    for i in range(nb_epoch):
        model.fit(X, y, epochs=1, batch_size=batch_size, verbose=1,
shuffle=False)
        model.reset_states()
```

```python
    return model

# make a one-step forecast
def forecast_lstm(model, batch_size, X):
    X = X.reshape(1, 1, len(X))
    yhat = model.predict(X, batch_size=batch_size)
    return yhat[0,0]

#LSTM Training model
data = (cluster_values[:,0] + cluster_values[:,1])/2
supervised = timeseries_to_supervised(data, 1)
supervised_values = supervised.values

test_size = 100

train_lstm, test_lstm = supervised_values[0:-test_size],
supervised_values[-test_size:]
# transform the scale of the data
scaler, train_scaled_lstm, test_scaled_lstm = scale(train_lstm,
test_lstm)

# fit the model batch,Epoch,Neurons
lstm_model = fit_lstm(train_scaled_lstm, 1, 50 , 64)
# forecast the entire training dataset to build up state for
forecasting
train_reshaped = train_scaled_lstm[:,
0].reshape(len(train_scaled_lstm), 1, 1)

from matplotlib import pyplot
import matplotlib.pyplot as plt
from tqdm import tqdm
from matplotlib.patches import Ellipse

predictions = list()
predictions_std_test = list()

for i in tqdm(range(0, len(test_scaled_lstm))):
    # make one-step forecast
    X, y = test_scaled_lstm[i, 0:-1], test_scaled_lstm[i, -1]

    stats = []
    for x in range(10):
        yhat = forecast_lstm(lstm_model, 1, X)
        # invert scaling
        yhat = invert_scale(scaler, X, yhat)
        stats.append(yhat)
    stats = np.array(stats)
    yhat = stats.mean()
```

```python
    yhat_std = stats.std()

    # store forecast
    predictions.append(yhat)
    predictions_std_test.append(yhat_std)
    expected = k_values[len(train_lstm) + i]

threshold = 3
anomly_location = []
for x in range(len(predictions_std_test)):
    if predictions_std_test[x] > threshold:
        print(x)
        anomly_location.append(x)

##graphs
# line plot of observed vs predicted
figsize=(12, 12)
fig, axs = plt.subplots(2,figsize=figsize)


axs[0].plot(data[-test_size:],color='blue',label='Actuals')
axs[0].plot(predictions,'r-',label='Predicted')

anomly_index=0
for loc in anomly_location:
    anomly_index+=1
    circle = Ellipse((loc, predictions[loc]), width=5, height=7.5 ,
color='pink',alpha=0.7, fill=True, label=f'Anomly location
{anomly_index}')
    axs[0].add_patch(circle)

axs[1].plot(predictions_std_test,'--',label='Predicted_std')
y = threshold
axs[1].axhline(y=y, color='r', linestyle='--',label='threshold')
axs[0].legend(loc='upper left')
axs[1].legend(loc='upper left')

# axs[0].set_ylim([1,12])
axs[0].set_xlabel('time * 2 min')
axs[1].set_xlabel('time * 2 min')
axs[1].set_ylabel('standard deviation value')
axs[1].grid(True)
plt.savefig('Anomly_loc.png')
plt.show()
```

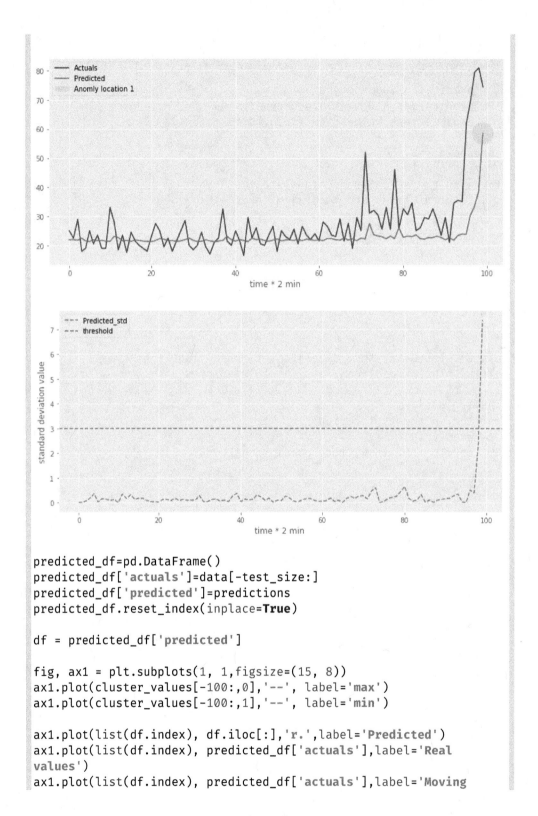

```
predicted_df=pd.DataFrame()
predicted_df['actuals']=data[-test_size:]
predicted_df['predicted']=predictions
predicted_df.reset_index(inplace=True)

df = predicted_df['predicted']

fig, ax1 = plt.subplots(1, 1,figsize=(15, 8))
ax1.plot(cluster_values[-100:,0],'--', label='max')
ax1.plot(cluster_values[-100:,1],'--', label='min')

ax1.plot(list(df.index), df.iloc[:],'r.',label='Predicted')
ax1.plot(list(df.index), predicted_df['actuals'],label='Real
values')
ax1.plot(list(df.index), predicted_df['actuals'],label='Moving
```

```
Average')
ax1.plot(list(df.index),
df.rolling(window=3).mean(),'r',label='Moving Average')

mu = df.rolling(window=3).mean()
sigma = df.rolling(window=3).std()
one_sigma_pos = mu+sigma
one_sigma_neg = mu-sigma
two_sigma_pos = mu+2*sigma
two_sigma_neg = mu-2*sigma
three_sigma_pos = mu+3*sigma
three_sigma_neg = mu-3*sigma

ax1.fill_between(df.index, one_sigma_pos, one_sigma_neg
,color='pink',alpha=0.5,label='1-Sigma')
ax1.fill_between(df.index, two_sigma_pos, two_sigma_neg
,color='pink',alpha=0.4,label='2-Sigma')
ax1.fill_between(df.index, three_sigma_pos, three_sigma_neg
,color='pink',alpha=0.3,label='3-Sigma')

ax1.set_xlabel('time * 2 min')
ax1.set_ylabel('Cluster size')
ax1.set_title('Data prediction for last 200 min')
ax1.legend();
plt.savefig('mu-sigma.png')
plt.show()
```

```
#https://datascience.stackexchange.com/questions/42715/how-to-
calculate-prediction-error-in-a-lstm-keras
#https://medium.com/hal24k-techblog/how-to-generate-neural-network-
confidence-intervals-with-keras-e4c0b78ebbdf
#Step-6, Getting anomly location and saving it back to csv file
```

```python
#1 is its anomalous
#0 if its not
#prediction on full data
predictions = list()
predictions_std = list()

for i in tqdm(range(0, len(train_scaled_lstm))):
    # make one-step forecast
    X, y = train_scaled_lstm[i, 0:-1], train_scaled_lstm[i, -1]

    stats = []
    for x in range(10):
        yhat = forecast_lstm(lstm_model, 1, X)
        # invert scaling
        yhat = invert_scale(scaler, X, yhat)
        stats.append(yhat)
    stats = np.array(stats)
    yhat = stats.mean()
    yhat_std = stats.std()

    # store forecast
    predictions.append(yhat)
    predictions_std.append(yhat_std)

final_anomly_location = []
for x in range(len(predictions_std)):
    if predictions_std[x] > threshold:
        print(x)
        final_anomly_location.append(x)
anomly_location_in_test = [x+len(train_scaled_lstm) for x in
anomly_location]

final_anomly_location.extend(anomly_location_in_test)
print(final_anomly_location)

anomly_list =
np.array([0]*(len(train_scaled_lstm)+len(test_scaled_lstm)))
anomly_list[final_anomly_location]=1

#Anomaly Plots
predictions_std.extend(predictions_std_test)
plt.figure(figsize=(16,6))
plt.plot(predictions_std)
for i in final_anomly_location:
    plt.axvspan(i,i+1, alpha=0.3, color='yellow')
plt.xlabel('Time steps')
plt.ylabel('Anomaly Score / predictions std')
```

```python
plt.savefig('aggregated anomaly score.png')
plt.show()
```

```python
print(anomly_list)

#####Final suspected columns
suspected_columns = []
for x in range(len(anomly_list)):
    if anomly_list[x] == 1:
        print(dic_col_relation[x])
        r = list(range(dic_col_relation[x]['start'],
dic_col_relation[x]['end']))
        suspected_columns.extend(r)
##Auto-Encoder part for more precision on rows
from sklearn.model_selection import train_test_split
#Data-generation for normal casses - Convert classes to Integer
df = pd.read_csv("log.csv")      #csv file with random time added
df['Level'] = pd.factorize(df['Level'])[0] + 1
df['EventId'] = pd.factorize(df['EventId'])[0] + 1
df['Component'] = pd.factorize(df['Component'])[0] + 1
df['EventTemplate'] = pd.factorize(df['EventTemplate'])[0] + 1
suspected_data=[]
for rows in tqdm(range(df.shape[0])):
    if rows in suspected_columns:
        tdf = df[['Pid', 'Level', 'Component', 'EventId',
'EventTemplate']].iloc[rows].values
        tdf = np.append(tdf, sen2vec[rows])
        suspected_data.append(tdf)

suspected_data = np.array(suspected_data)
suspected_data.shape

scaler = MinMaxScaler(feature_range=(-1, 1))
scaler = scaler.fit(suspected_data)
suspected_data_scaled = scaler.transform(suspected_data)
nb_epoch = 50
batch_size = 1
```

```python
input_dim = suspected_data_scaled.shape[1]
learning_rate = 1e-4

input_layer = Input(shape=(input_dim, ))
encoder = Dense(128, activation="tanh",
activity_regularizer=regularizers.l1(learning_rate))(input_layer)
encoder = Dense(64, activation="relu")(encoder)
encoder = Dense(8, activation="relu")(encoder)

decoder = Dense(8, activation='tanh')(encoder)
decoder = Dense(64, activation='tanh')(decoder)
decoder = Dense(128, activation='tanh')(decoder)
decoder = Dense(input_dim, activation='linear')(decoder)

autoencoder = Model(inputs=input_layer, outputs=decoder)
autoencoder.summary()
autoencoder.compile(metrics=['accuracy'],loss='mse',optimizer='adam
')

history = autoencoder.fit(suspected_data_scaled,
suspected_data_scaled, epochs=nb_epoch, batch_size=batch_size,
                          shuffle=True,verbose=1).history
# validation_data=(test_x, test_x)

plt.plot(history['loss'], linewidth=2, label='loss')
plt.legend(loc='upper right')
plt.title('Model loss')
plt.ylabel('Loss')
plt.xlabel('Epoch')
plt.show()
```

```python
pred = autoencoder.predict(suspected_data_scaled)
mse = np.mean(np.power(suspected_data_scaled - pred, 2), axis=1)
plt.figure(figsize = (16,8))
plt.plot(mse, '--')
```

```
y = 2*np.mean(mse)
plt.axhline(y=y, color='b', linestyle='--',label='threshold')
plt.show()
```

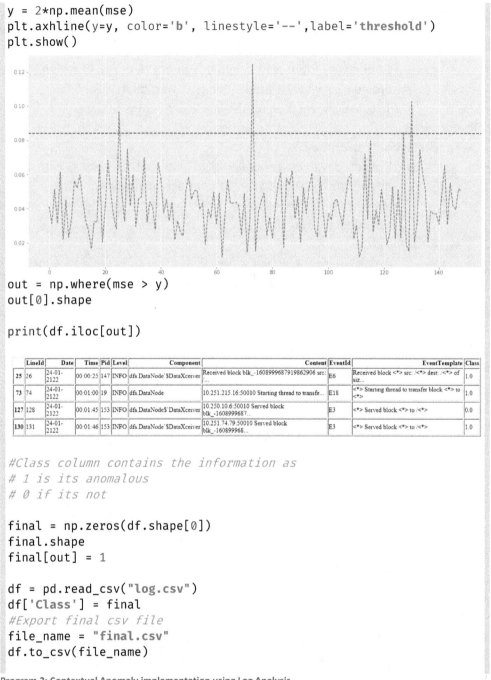

```
out = np.where(mse > y)
out[0].shape

print(df.iloc[out])
```

	LineId	Date	Time	Pid	Level	Component	Content	EventId	EventTemplate	Class
25	26	24-01-2122	00:00:25	147	INFO	dfs.DataNode`$DataXceiver	Received block blk_-1608999687919862906 src:/...	E6	Received block <*> src: /<*> dest: /<*> of siz...	1.0
73	74	24-01-2122	00:01:00	19	INFO	dfs.DataNode	10.251.215.16:50010 Starting thread to transfe...	E18	<*> Starting thread to transfer block <*> to <*>	1.0
127	128	24-01-2122	00:01:45	153	INFO	dfs.DataNode$`DataXceiver	10.250.10.6:50010 Served block blk_-1608999687...	E3	<*> Served block <*> to /<*>	0.0
130	131	24-01-2122	00:01:46	153	INFO	dfs.DataNode`$DataXceiver	10.251.74.79:50010 Served block blk_-160899968...	E3	<*> Served block <*> to /<*>	1.0

```
#Class column contains the information as
# 1 is its anomalous
# 0 if its not

final = np.zeros(df.shape[0])
final.shape
final[out] = 1

df = pd.read_csv("log.csv")
df['Class'] = final
#Export final csv file
file_name = "final.csv"
df.to_csv(file_name)
```

Program 2: Contextual Anomaly implementation using Log Analysis

Data which is outside the 3 standard deviations has been classified as anomaly. The Final.csv has the data along with the predicted anomaly.

Visualization:
- o The plot illustrates predicted values, actual values, and their respective moving averages.
- o Confidence intervals (1-sigma, 2-sigma, 3-sigma) are highlighted, providing a visual understanding of prediction reliability.
- o The analysis focuses on the last 200 minutes of data.

Observations
- **Prediction Performance:**
  - o Predicted values generally align with actual values, with some deviations highlighted by the confidence intervals.
  - o Variability increases over time, as seen in the widening of confidence intervals.
- **Error Insights:**
  - o Areas where the actual values lie outside the confidence intervals indicate significant prediction errors.

* * *

www.ingramcontent.com/pod-product-compliance
Lightning Source LLC
LaVergne TN
LVHW080115070326
832902LV00015B/2595